T0358498

ROUTLEDGE LIBRARY EDITIONS:
INTERNATIONAL BUSINESS

MULTINATIONALS AND ECONOMIC DEVELOPMENT

MULTINATIONALS AND ECONOMIC DEVELOPMENT
An integration of competing theories

JAMES C. W. AHIAKPOR

Volume 1

LONDON AND NEW YORK

First published in 1990

This edition first published in 2013
by Routledge
2 Park Square, Milton Park, Abingdon, Oxon, OX14 4RN

Simultaneously published in the USA and Canada
by Routledge
711 Third Avenue, New York, NY 10017

Routledge is an imprint of the Taylor & Francis Group, an informa business

British Library Cataloguing in Publication Data
A catalogue record for this book is available from the British Library

ISBN: 978-0-415-63009-2 (Set)
eISBN: 978-0-203-07716-0 (Set)
ISBN: 978-0-415-63920-0 (Volume 1)
eISBN: 978-0-203-02860-5 (Volume 1)

Publisher's Note
The publisher has gone to great lengths to ensure the quality of this reprint but
points out that some imperfections in the original copies may be apparent.

Disclaimer
The publisher has made every effort to trace copyright holders and would
welcome correspondence from those they have been unable to trace.

Printed and bound by CPI Group (UK) Ltd, Croydon, CR0 4YY

Multinationals and economic development

An integration of competing theories

James C.W. Ahiakpor

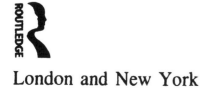

London and New York

First published 1990
by Routledge
11 New Fetter Lane, London EC4P 4EE

Simultaneously published in the USA and Canada
by Routledge
a division of Routledge, Chapman and Hall, Inc.
29 West 35th Street, New York, NY 10001

Phototypeset in 10pt Times by
Mews Photosetting. Beckenham, Kent
Printed and bound in Great Britain by
Biddles Ltd, Guildford and King's Lynn

British Library Cataloguing in Publication Data

Ahiakpor, James C.W. *1945–*
Multinationals and economic development : an integration
of competing theories. – (International business series).
1. Developing countries. Economic development. Role of
multinational companies
I. Title   II. Series
338.8881724

ISBN 0-415-02282-7

Library of Congress Cataloging in Publication Data

Ahiakpor, James C.W., 1945–
    Multinationals and economic development : an integration of
competing theories / James C.W. Ahiakpor.
        p.   cm. – (International business series)
    Includes bibliographical references and index.
    ISBN 0-415-02282-7
    1. International business enterprises – Developing countries.
2. Investments, Foreign – Developing countries. 3. Developing
countries – Economic policy. I. Title. II. Series: International
business series (London, England)
HD2932.A32   1990
338.8′881724–dc20   90-37008
                                                         CIP

To my mother,
PAULA DOFI

Contents

Foreword

There is a saying that economics is too important to be left to economists. This book demonstrates that development economics is too important to be left to development economists.

For far too long students of the economics and politics of less-developed countries (LDCs) have lacked insight into the nature and extent of activities by multinational enterprises (MNEs). Yet MNEs today literally dominate world trade and direct investment patterns. For too long work on the MNE in LDCs has been clouded by a Marxist perspective on distribution rather than efficiency issues. The MNEs have been seen as too powerful and in need of regulation by governments of LDCs. Often the result has been continued poverty.

Professor James Ahiakpor brings a fresh approach to the analysis of MNEs in LDCs. His is the first study to integrate the modern theory of the MNE into the corpus of literature on economic development. Professor Ahiakpor explains how MNEs 'internalize' firm specific advantages as a perfectly normal type of economic activity. His focus is upon the efficiency aspects of MNEs. This leads him towards a new and more balanced view of the positive role of MNEs in economic development. He argues that the issue of the transfer of technology to LDCs can only be understood by knowledge of the managerial characteristics and techniques of the MNE, not just by a one-sided demand for appropriate technology by LDCs. He is not in favour of a simplistic approach towards government regulation of the MNE.

In these times of rapid political change and increased questioning of the doctrines of Marxism, it is refreshing to have this new view of economic development. A sound analysis of the performance of MNEs can only be of value to the governments of LDCs. It is important to know that MNEs earn normal rates of return and do not make excessive profits on their activities in LDCs. It is important to know that MNEs contribute to exports and are not simply in import-competing sectors. It is important to have a balanced view of the contribution of MNEs towards economic development. Professor Ahiakpor was a man ahead of his time when writing this book; now he has a book relevant for today's debate about the future of MNEs in LDCs.

ALAN M. RUGMAN
University of Toronto

Preface

My purpose in writing this book is to integrate as much as possible valid aspects of the competing theories or hypotheses about the role of foreign firms, particularly multinational corporations (MNCs), in the economic growth and development process of host less-developed countries (LDCs). It is an ambitious task given the huge amount of research output that exists on the role of multinationals in the process of economic development. It is also a difficult task since I seek to derive from the exercise conclusions that will assist the formulation of more consistent policies for economic development in the Third World. Much of the difficulty arises from the fact that policymaking appears to be driven more by ideological commitments than by the pursuit of logical consistency. However, I hope that by presenting my arguments in the nature of competing policy options and their consequences for host countries, many of the inconsistent arguments and policies that have been urged or adopted in the Third World can be discarded.

The main conclusion I reach from my attempts to integrate both theoretical and empirical research is that foreign firms, including multinationals, are better regarded as neutral agents in the process of economic growth and development. Whether they contribute positively or negatively to the development process depends very much on the economic policy climate within which they operate. Granted financial inducements to invest within a regime of market distortions created by other government policies, these firms may not contribute much (if at all) to the economic growth or development of host countries other than in the sectors in which they operate. However, if treated like other privately owned firms in the host countries, and within a regime characterized by freedom of private enterprise, foreign firms may contribute significantly to economic growth and development. Their contributions have to be measured primarily in terms of the opportunities they present for domestic factor owners to earn higher incomes than might otherwise be possible.

To set other criteria upon which to judge the contributions of foreign firms, including MNCs, is to embark on a frustrating course both for host governments and the firms. Such frustration may cause foreign firms to curtail or withdraw investments from countries whose policies demand that they divert attention and resources away from their main goal of earning the maximum profits possible. The governments, on the other hand, may find the reactions of foreign firms bewildering, but it is the economies of the host countries that suffer from a denial of opportunities for mutually beneficial voluntary exchange between owners of foreign firms and local factors of production that could have been purchased or hired.

Of course, the argument that foreign firms, including MNCs, should be treated just like any other private local firms with respect to incentives is not new. That policy has long been urged, especially by analysts critical of MNC activities in LDCs. However, the basis of their conclusion is that by engaging in competitive bidding for investment from MNCs LDCs give away much of the financial advantage they otherwise might have received. They would rather have LDCs unite against MNCs to extract monopsony gains from their investments. Otherwise, using an agency such as the United Nations, LDCs might seek to regulate the earnings of MNCs to assure themselves better development prospects.

The basis for my conclusion is different from the above. It stems from a recognition of the purposive behaviour of foreign and locally owned firms. Both types of firms seek to maximize profits from their investments. Financial inducements paid by the government (out of domestic factor incomes) thus may not increase total national income. But neither would the restraints on foreign firms being sought at the international level.

The profit-seeking argument for treating both foreign and local firms alike with respect to incentives is also not new. It is rooted in the premises of classical and early neoclassical economists such as Adam Smith, David Ricardo, John Stuart Mill, and Alfred Marshall in advocating a neutralist or *laissez-faire* policy with respect to business incentives or restraints. The classical premises also render redundant the requirement of perfect competition for adopting a neutalist policy. Departure from their arguments by modern neoclassical or welfare economists has tended to leave economic policy prescriptions quite untidy. I hope that a renewed emphasis on the classical premises will promote better economic modelling and policy prescription regarding MNCs and economic development in LDCs.

JAMES C.W. AHIAKPOR
Department of Economics
Saint Mary's University
Halifax, Nova Scotia, Canada

Acknowledgements

This book might not have appeared at this time but for the kind encouragement I have received from the series editor, Professor Alan Rugman. I am most grateful to him for alerting me to the opportunity. He brought to my attention the need for integrating both the theory and empirical research on multinationals and economic development in the Third World. I evidently caught his attention with my paper, 'The profits of foreign firms in a less developed country: Ghana', presented in 1984 at the Administrative Sciences Association of Canada Conference, demonstrating that foreign firms do not make excessive profits in LDCs as Marxists or dependency-theory adherents have argued.

Professor Rugman has since borne my numerous requests for extending the deadline for submitting the manuscript as I have been unable to resist trying to complete other research projects that appeared to be demanding even more of my immediate attention. An example is my three-year effort to convince several doubting reviewers for journals that the main reason John Maynard Keynes inverted the long-standing theory of interest rate determination, from Adam Smith to Alfred Marshall, was his having misinterprted the classical fund concept of 'capital' to mean capital goods. (The article is now scheduled for publication in the *History of Political Economy* in 1990.) Some of the other distractions are quite relevant to the main issues I discuss in this book, as will become evident from the text.

Professor Rugman also has read and offered valuable comments on some of the chapters. Peter Sowden, and later Andrew Lockett, who have been the Social Science Editors of Croom Helm and Routledge, respectively, have also been patient with my delays. Mr Sowden also assisted me with some relevant research materials. I am grateful for their understanding.

I also thank Professor Diery Seck. He has read several of the chapters and offered valuable criticisms. We still retain some of our differences on the issues I discuss here, but I think my reactions to his comments have helped to improve my presentation. I extend the same gratitude to several anonymous readers of my articles published in *Economic Development and Cultural Change* (1989b) and the *Journal of Development Economics* (1986) the substance of which bear closely on my discussions in this book.

Dr Robert Lipsey generously sent me some helpful publications and working papers on productivity studies written by some members of the NBER, of which he is the New York director. I thank him. I would also like to thank Professor Gerald Helleiner for assisting me with some research materials, including his own publications. He was equally generous with his time and guidance when I wrote my 1981 doctoral dissertation on multinationals at the University of Toronto. Much of the insight for this research derives from that work. Needless to say, Gerry and I do not necessarily share the same policy conclusions.

Finally, I thank Miss Bernadine Halliday and Miss Roxane Krulicki for their assistance in compiling and typing the bibliography. A personal computer made available for me by the Dean of Commerce Faculty has saved me from burdening others with my numerous revisions of the manuscript.

None of the above is responsible for any shortcomings of the book. I am alone to blame for those.

Chapter one

Introduction

The passion previously generated by debate over the activities of multinational corporations (MNCs) in the less-developed countries (LDCs) has now subsided considerably. The positive role these firms can play in the development process of host LDCs is now generally admitted, even if grudgingly by some. However, many still urge close supervision and restraints on the activities of MNCs lest they exploit LDC economies.[1] There is thus much room for clarifying the theories of foreign direct investment and the process of economic development to permit a more healthy attitude towards foreign firms and the adoption of more consistent policies for Third World economic development. Part of that effort entails the restatement of some fundamental concepts from the classical and early neoclassical economists that have evidently become distorted over time. Another avenue is to interpret empirical research findings within a more consistent theoretical framework.

At one time the direct investment activities of foreign firms came under a storm of criticism, mainly from Marxist academics, proponents of the dependency theory of underdevelopment, and partly from some LDC governments.[2] The title of Raymond Vernon's 1977 book, *Storm Over the Multinationals*, accurately describes this state of affairs. To many Marxists the very presence of MNCs in the Third World could not be conducive to the economic development of LDCs. Such firms were or still are seen to be instruments of international capitalist exploitation. Economic development, according to these critics, could only come from investment of indigenous capital, preferably under the control of the state. These arguments became popular during the late 1960s and early 1970s, almost in direct contradiction to earlier theories of foreign direct investment which emphasized mainly the positive contributions of foreign firms to economic development.

Not all governments critical of the activities of multinational corporations in their countries ascribed to Marxist or dependency theory arguments. Many may have intended by such criticisms either to extract

1

more economic benefits from foreign firms or to minimize the influences of such firms they considered as obstacles to their political goals.

By the mid-1970s, inconsistencies in both the criticisms and praise of the activities of foreign firms in LDCs had become quite glaring, as depicted in the introductory paragraph of an article in *The Economist* (24 January 1976, p. 68):

> It [the MNC] fiddles its accounts. It avoids or evades its taxes. It rigs its intra-company transfer prices. It is run by foreigners, from decision centres thousands of miles away. It imports foreign labour practices. It doesn't import foreign labour practices. It overpays. It underpays. It competes unfairly with local firms. It is in cahoots with local firms. It exports jobs from rich countries. It is an instrument of rich countries imperialism. The technologies it brings to the third world are old-fashioned. No, they are too modern. It meddles. It bribes. Nobody can control it. It plays off governments against each other to get the biggest incentives. Won't it please come and invest? Let it bloody well go home.

Some of the negative claims about activities of foreign firms, particularly MNCs, also form the basis of a set of resolutions adopted by the Sixth Special Session of the United Nations General Assembly in 1974, commonly known as the New International Economic Order (NIEO). Among the proposed actions intended to promote greater development in the Third World are regulation of the conduct of MNCs and the establishment of mechanisms for the transfer of appropriate technology from the more-developed to the less-developed countries.[3] A clearer understanding of the role of foreign firms in economic development and a greater appreciation of the purposive behaviour of individuals, including those of the Third World, might have spared much of the inconsistencies in the policy recommendations of this and other documents it later inspired.

The criticisms of MNC activities in LDCs and adoption of resolutions to manage foreign direct investment at a global level may be interpreted as reflecting the failure of relevant theories of the firm and economic development to explain issues clearly. A vast amount of the theoretical literature on foreign direct investment takes the form of attempting to fill a perceived gap in the traditional textbook theory of the firm which explains, albeit inadequately, the activities of firms operating within their own countries.[4] According to this theory, sales abroad are supposed to be conducted as part of the international exchange of goods and services, not movements of plant, equipment, and personnel. Thus the theory of foreign direct investment has been founded on the absence of perfect competition in product as well as factor markets.

However, theories of foreign direct investment based on market imperfections have their own limitations for guiding good and consistent policymaking. Modern welfare economics, which came into prominence in the late 1930s, accepts non-intervention by governments directly in the marketplace to promote community welfare (if it can be measured) only if there is perfect competition in both the product and input markets (see for example, Bator 1957).[5] The very absence of perfect competition thus seems to suggest that unless regulated by governments, the activities of firms, particularly foreign-owned ones, do not promote the greatest increases in the welfare of communities in which they operate.

Yet many contributors to the theory of foreign direct investment emphasize the negative consequences government regulation of foreign firms can have for economic growth in host countries. They argue that MNCs are efficient contributors to economic growth because they are able to internalize market imperfections. That is, they create efficient internal markets to replace what is missing in the arms-length, external market (see, for example, Casson 1982; Rugman 1980, 1986).

To critics of MNCs, such arguments provide little assurance that foreign firms would not extract excessive incomes or rents from LDC economies through the mechanism of internalization. They might even quote Adam Smith, the doyen of free-market or *laissez-faire* policies, who wrote some harsh comments on merchants and 'master manufacturers'. Warning that policy proposals from such groups should be listened to with 'great precaution', Smith (1976: 278) called them a group 'whose interest is never exactly the same with that of the public, who have generally an interest to deceive and even to oppress the public, and who accordingly have, upon many occasions, both deceived and oppressed it'. Unless interpreted correctly in the context in which Smith wrote them, his comments would appear to undermine the policy of free enterprise and support instead arguments for government intervention. That is, governments must act as protectors of the public interest through regulation of the activities of foreign firms.[6]

My approach in this book is to clarify the theory of the firm without invoking the notion of market imperfections to explain the motivation for foreign direct investment or the emergence of multinational corporations. Coupled with the recognition that foreign firms contribute to economic growth through their purchases of local factors of production, including human capital, the imperfect-markets argument for restraining the activities of MNCs can be rendered redundant.

Many empirical tests of the negative claims made against foreign firms have failed to confirm them. These claims include the alleged exploitation of local labour, adoption of excessively capital-intensive techniques, non-responsiveness to local factor market conditions, choice of inappropriate technology, extraction of development capital through repatriation of excessive profits, and the creation of inappropriate tastes in the Third World. Indeed, the evaporation of the strong emotions that previously surrounded discussions of MNC activities in LDCs is largely due to the results of such empirical tests.

However, as is well known, bad theories in the social sciences are not readily discarded because of the failure of evidence to confirm them, and reluctance to discard such theories is also strengthened when the testing methods may be subject to valid criticisms, as are some of the empirical tests. Weaknesses of the tests include high degrees of aggregation across industries and ownership categories, and differences in the measurement of some important variables such as capital and factor productivity. Often the data are unreliable. But in spite of these weaknesses, many of the empirical studies have made careful interpretations of the evidence consistent with good logic. I believe that integrating their main conclusions with the theoretical literature has good potential for helping to resolve several of the remaining doubts about the positive role of foreign direct investment in the economic development of LDCs.

A few caveats may be in order before I embark on detailed discussion of the issues in the following chapters. First, I use the terms foreign firms and multinational corporations interchangeably in this book. MNCs are, in fact, a subset of foreign firms, although they are often much larger than the others, but I adopt this interchange of terms because most of the empirical studies I discuss do not distinguish between them. Indeed, few statistical sources report data separately for MNCs and other foreign firms. Anyhow, for the focus of this book, that is, determining the consequences of MNC activities for economic development, not much is lost from combining the two groups of firms; both contribute to economic development (or fail to do so) by how much income they create for local factors of production.

I also concentrate my analysis here on the development impact of foreign firms in LDCs. Much of the framework of my analysis is applicable to the more-developed countries (MDCs) as well, but attempting to extend the discussion to MDCs might dilute the focus unnecessarily. Most people, including academics and politicians, in those countries seem to appreciate more the economic benefits of foreign investment than appears to be the case in LDCs.

Finally, because I have given a detailed summary of the substantive chapters at the end of the book I shall skip the usual readers' guide in the introductory chapter. Suffice it to say that the rest of the book examines and reinterprets within the tenets of classical and early neoclassical economics theories of the firm, including multinationals, the role of firms in economic development, notions of appropriate technology, the role of exports in economic development, and government policies to promote efficient economic development.

Chapter two

The multinational corporation: a type of firm

Much confusion in the debate over the role of multinational corporations in economic development stems from their being perceived as a special kind of firm whose behaviour cannot be understood within the known theories of the firm. However, the main feature which distinguishes the MNC from other firms whose production and marketing activities are concentrated within one country, lies in its operations across different national boundaries. Thus, essentials of the standard theory of the firm apply equally to an MNC. These essentials are discussed here.

In its simplest conception, the firm is an institutional arrangement within which factors that may co-operate to produce goods and services for which there is, or perceived to be, demand are organized in a fairly stable relationship. The factors include capital (both financial and physical), labour, and land. Owners of these factors face an information gap, that is, knowing where, and in what quantities, their services are required in exchange for some (financial) reward – interest, dividends, wages, and rent. This information gap is mainly closed by an entrepreneur who undertakes the organizing function, thus constituting a firm.

The role of the entrepreneur is not just that of bridging the information gap. It includes the equally important role of assuming the risk that enough revenues, that is, above the costs of inputs, may not be forthcoming to pay the promised rewards. The organization (firm) collapses, with impairment to the wealth of the owners of participating (financial) capital, if revenues are persistently inadequate to meet expenditures. But a surplus of revenues over costs yields returns to the risks taken by the entrepreneur and others whose (financial) capitals co-operate in the venture.

The arrangement by which factors of production may co-operate to produce goods and services for some return could be sufficiently loose as to terminate after one day, one week, one month, or after the cycle of production is completed – from the beginning of processing of intermediate goods till they are ready for sale. However, the modern firm typically assumes a much longer life in order to overcome the inefficiency and costliness of frequent re-contracting among the factors. The contractual arrangement under which a firm exists thus provides some guarantee of income to the participating factors of production in the form of a binding contract to purchase their services over some specified period at some agreed fees. However, the entrepreneur and owners of participating financial capital (shareholders) have no such guarantees of income; their rewards vary with the fortunes of the firm.

The entrepreneur – the principal risk-taker – can hardly be acting solely to create income-earning opportunities for the hired factors of production. Rather, that such incomes are earned (in the form of interest, dividends, rent, and wages) is a secondary, yet evidently desirable, outcome of the primary motive of the risk-taker, namely, to earn profits. Of course, this is a motive which is very hard to confirm by interviewing firms directly. Anticipating, perhaps correctly, that the public would regard the pursuit of profits as evil, many entrepreneurs may deny that they are led into business by such a motive.[1]

Nevertheless, if the entrepreneur knew beforehand that after the cost of raw materials, interest, rent, wages, and taxes have been paid nothing would be left as a reward for the toil and trouble of organizing the enterprise, production would hardly take place. Thus, profits are the sustaining factor in the life of a firm. Without them the organizational function of the entrepreneur would cease, along with the demand for other factors of production, including the capitals of savers.[2]

A correct appreciation of the positive role of profits in sustaining productive enterprises is important in understanding the contributions of entrepreneurs to economic development. Such an appreciation underlies Adam Smith's pertinent observation:

> [M]an has almost constant occasion for the help of his brethen, and it is in vain for him to expect it from their benevolence only. He will be more likely to prevail if he can interest their self-love in his favour, and show them that it is for their own advantage to do for him what he requires of them. Whoever offers to another a bargain of any kind, proposes to do this. Give me that which I want, and you shall have this which you want, is the meaning of every such offer; and it is in this manner that we obtain from one another the far greater part of those good offices which we stand in need of. It is *not from the benevolence* of the butcher, the brewer, or the baker, that we expect our dinner, *but from their regard to their own interest*. We address ourselves, not to their humanity but to their self-love, and never talk to them of our own necessities but of their advantage.
>
> (Smith 1976: 18; my emphasis)

When profit-making by the firm is perceived in the same light as the self-interested drive of the labourer to seek employment at the highest wage possible, the saver to lend his capital at the highest interest obtainable, or the land- or equipment-owner to rent or lease to the highest bidder, a whole different set of industrial policies is engendered. They differ substantially from those conceived on the basis that profit-making is mainly a reflection of the evil of humankind (in the entrepreneur). In the study of the multinational corporation, such an appreciation of the role of profits in sustaining an enterprise assumes even greater importance.

The above description of the firm combines the functions of risk-taking and management of the productive enterprise into one entity: the entrepreneur. But that combination exists only within small-scale, owner-operated enterprises. Efficient though many such enterprises are, they suffer the handicaps of limited management expertise, limited scale on account of their owners' inability to raise much capital (own savings or bank credit), great uncertainty of survival, etc., since they rely mainly on the resources of their owners. Although somewhat minimized, these restrictions on the efficiency and size of firms affect partnerships as well. Thus, it is among those firms in which there is clear separation of ownership from entrepreneurial and management functions that multinationals belong.

The capital fund of most modern limited liability corporations is contributed by a large number of individuals through their purchase of shares. This fact alone tends to assure a larger size for such corporations, compared with owner-operated (single proprietorships) and partnership firms. Although such share purchases expose their owners to the risk of insufficient returns on their capital, their risk is different from that assumed by those who perform the entrepreneurial–organizational functions necessary for the success and survival of the enterprise.

Such functions are performed mainly by the few top managers (executives) who engage in the planning and supervision of the operations of the firm. In return, these individuals receive residual incomes akin to those earned by the owner-operators of small enterprises. In times of high profits their incomes rise (bonuses and participating shares), and they also suffer diminution in incomes or lose their jobs in times of great losses.

Lewellen (1969) illustrates this point very well. Using data on fifty of the largest US public corporations over the period 1940–63, he found that:

(a) total remuneration of top executives fluctuated sharply along with the market value of company stocks (his proxy for profits);
(b) stock-based rewards contributed between 20 and 50 per cent of the after-tax earnings of senior executives;
(c) per capita average stockholdings of such executives amounted to between $2 and $3 million (from 1960 to 1963); and

(d) the average ratio of the sum of dividends, capital gains, and stock-based compensation to the 'traditional fixed-dollar rewards' (salaries) of the top corporate executives ranged between 4 and 5. That is, salaries were about one-fifth the total remuneration of top executives.

Furthermore, his data reveal a growing trend towards stock-based rewards and away from fixed-dollar payments (salaries) for top corporate executives.

Other performers of the entrepreneurial function, including risk-bearing, are those who constitute the board of directors (some of whom are the executive managers of the corporation). They also risk their capital by individually owning shares in the corporation, and thus take an active part in planning and supervising the operations of the firm. The board thus serves as a supervisory agent on behalf of the majority of shareholders who, because of the size and complexity of the modern corporation, cannot individually participate directly in the decision-making of the firm.[3]

Finally, within the modern large corporation there are the hired managers who implement decisions of the executive, normally for guaranteed rewards or salaries. Though the rewards of such managers may rise with their performance (bonuses and promotion), their fortunes are less directly tied to the fortunes of the firm than those of the entrepreneur–manager group.

Thus, in spite of its complexity, the modern large corporation, of which the multinational enterprise is but one type, retains the basic features of the firm described above. It is an organization within which, for some specified fees, factors of production are organized and directed by an entrepreneurial group who receive mainly residual incomes or share of profits.

Failure to perceive correctly the role of the entrepreneur–manager group within a firm as distinct from the capital-supplying function of shareholders appears to have led to the so-called 'agency problem' associated with large corporations. The argument is that there is separation of ownership from control in the modern large corporation. That separation, it is alleged, makes it possible for management to pursue their own interests which may be quite inconsistent with the profit-maximizing goals of the owners (shareholders).[4] But the argument largely ignores the fact that shareholders are, in effect, only lenders of capital to the firm. Many of them have no management or organizational skills. They have chosen deliberately to entrust their savings to entre-preneurs in anticipation of sharing in the profits they expect the firm to make. Upon being disappointed, or on the appearance of more promising prospects of greater returns elsewhere, these capital-lenders often divest themselves of the poorer performing shares. The interests of entrepreneurs, on the other hand, include both the profitability and long-term survival of the firm.[5]

The above conception of the firm is in general consistent with Coase's rationale for the existence of the firm, with some differences of emphasis. Instead of the dominance of the profit motive, Coase (1937) lays more emphasis on the view that 'there is a cost of using the price mechanism' (p. 390), the avoidance of which leads entrepreneurs to 'organize' firms. He thus suggests that 'the distinguishing mark of the firm is the supersession of the price mechanism' (p. 389). However, the purpose of avoiding the transactions cost associated with using the open market or arm's-length transactions ultimately must be to raise the net revenue of the firm. Thus, profit-making being the primary motive of the firm can be inferred from Coase's explanation of what brings the firm into existence.

However, Coase's 'distinguishing mark of the firm', namely, the attempt to supersede the price mechanism, can be misleading.[6] Although it connotes the internalization of some market activities that otherwise would have been conducted at arm's-length, the reward system within a firm is still greatly influenced by the price mechanism – the notion of opportunity costs explicitly or implicitly employed by the parties involved in contracting. Furthermore, this view may lend itself to being (mis)used to make the argument that firms tend to substitute for, or replace the market mechanism, with some deleterious consequences for 'community welfare'.

Such an interpretation could hardly be Coase's intent. In the 1937 article, he also contrasts the greater efficiency of private enterprise with state intervention in the form of economic planning. The latter is 'imposed on industry while firms arise voluntarily because they represent a more efficient method of organizing production', he says, adding: 'In a competitive system, there is an "optimal" amount of planning!'[7]

The description of the firm I adopt here also retains the significance of the nature of income receipts in identifying the organizer of a firm, but which Coase (1937: 392–3) minimizes. Contrary to his view, entrepreneurs do not sell their services for 'a certain sum of money'. Rather, they are those who perceive profitable opportunities and risk their wealth and the capitals of others, to hire the services of other factors of production (for a certain sum of money) in expectation of an uncertain, residual income. Failure to maintain this distinction may lead to considerable difficulty in recognizing 'the firm', as encountered, for example, in Cheung (1983).

Aside from these qualifications, much of the description of the firm employed in this chapter is consistent with its conception by Coase (1937: 386):

> a definition of a firm . . . which is not only realistic in that it corresponds to what is meant by a firm in the real world, but is

tractable by two of the most powerful instruments of economic analysis developed by [Alfred] Marshall, the idea of the margin and that of substitution, together giving the idea of substitution at the margin.

Comparing uninational and multinational corporations

The above description of the firm is sufficiently general to explain the behaviour of both domestic or uninational corporations (UNCs) and multinational corporations. The basic aim pursued by both of these enterprises is to sell what they produce for the most net revenue. They both could sell their products on the wholesale market, in which case they would deal with intermediaries who in turn sell their products in the retail market. Indeed, some of the products of the uninational firm may be sold abroad by retailers. The first basic difference between UNCs and MNCs thus arises from the fact that one concentrates production and sale in a single country while the other engages in these same activities in more than one country. Nevertheless, they both use the market process to attain their profit-making goals.

The UNC may also establish branch plants in different regions of the same country, regions which could have been separated by international boundaries. Indeed, regions in some countries are even more geographically separated (e.g. the islands of Japan or the Philippines, and mainland United States of America from Alaska and Hawaii) than are many contiguous countries. A firm becomes a multinational merely by locating production plants across national borders, for example, between Canada and the US, the US and Mexico, France and Spain, or Germany and Switzerland. But even within the same nation, particularly in a federal state, rights and obligations, including tax laws, under which the UNC operates may differ across regions.

Another aspect of the jurisdictional distinction is the currency (the medium of exchange) within which transactions are conducted. Only in a few circumstances will a currency unit be acceptable across international boundaries.[8] The significance of this distinction also may be blurred by the use of forward exchange markets to eliminate the impact of day-to-day fluctuations of exchange rates on the operations of the MNC. On the other hand, the UNC may also be exposed to the impact of international currency fluctuations on those inputs it purchases from abroad.

Much of the theoretical literature on the multinational corporation is concerned with attempting to explain why they establish plants in foreign countries rather than only at home, and contrasts their behaviour with uninational firms whose products may yet be marketed abroad. The explanations differ mainly in some minor detail from those which explain why a firm establishes production plants in different regions of the same country.

For both UNCs and MNCs, multi-plant production must be more profitable than a single-plant production. This may be due to differential subsidies or taxes (tariffs) imposed on the sale of products manufactured outside a region or country. This is one of the means governments (local or national) adopt in their attempt to create employment within their jurisdictions. The subsidy or tariff raises revenues for firms producing for sale within the region while reducing revenues for those which produce outside the region or country.

Similarly, just as the entrepreneur attempts to eliminate the uncertainty with securing the desired services of some factors of production, e.g. labour, by entering into a contractual arrangement, a multinational corporation may establish a raw-materials production or processing plant in a foreign country if arm's-length purchases from foreign sellers are unreliable. Furthermore, it may be more difficult to sue successfully for breach of supply contracts against suppliers located in a foreign country than within the same country. It is potential costs such as these (irregularity of supply or difficulty of contract enforcement) that the MNC may seek to eliminate by locating abroad.

By the same token, unreliability of supplies from input sellers in the domestic market may cause the UNC to establish input production or processing plants in different regions of the same country, especially if costs of enforcing supply contracts are considered high. It is another case in which the costliness of arm's-length transactions affects the nature or organization of a firm's production, as well as its size, as argued in Coase (1937).

In both cases, what is replaced by locating input processing plants in different regions or countries may be previous input suppliers. These also might have bought primary raw materials from domestic producers before processing or packaging for sale to the final producer, the UNC or MNC. Locating input processing plants abroad may thus increase competition for the purchase of primary raw materials from local producers. Even if MNCs take over controlling interest in local firms from which they previously purchased materials (vertical integration), there is no elimination of the market for primary raw materials.

Rarely does the establishment of an input production plant by a UNC or MNC completely eliminate production of primary products by their traditional suppliers. But if such elimination did occur, most or all of the traditional producers probably would be hired by the new firm. If so, there would have been a substitution of markets, the labour market for a product (raw materials) market.

It might also be more profitable to locate a production plant in a different region or country rather than importing raw materials for processing if the materials lose considerable weight during processing. The relevant explanation for a firm being a multinational rather than a uninational in such a case would have to be based on the type of products it sells, and in which market. Indeed we find a greater concentration of MNCs in some industries than in others.

Another common distinction frequently drawn between UNCs and MNCs is the degree of research and development (R&D) activities they undertake.[9] This distinction is meaningful primarily with respect to scale. Research may assist both UNCs and MNCs to discover more efficient ways of producing the same product. (Even in the case of a complete monopoly – sale of a good or service by a single seller – research to discover cheaper ways of production would aid profit-making by the firm.) Research may assist the firm to compete more effectively by varying the quality of goods and services it sells to better suit the perceived tastes and preferences of its customers. Research may also help the firm to discover ways in which it can reach a wider market through advertising. Only for highly standardized products (or services) would there be little reward from investing in research to improve product quality and/or methods of marketing.

Also, by its nature, outright sale of technology can hardly be profitable. Instead, technology may be embodied in the goods and services sold by a frm or in production processes. There may be difficulties of appropriating quickly adequate returns on newly developed knowledge – 'the problem of appropriability' (Magee 1981). There are also likely to be differences in the capitalized (subjective) values of the possible returns on new knowledge between its creators and potential buyers. Buyers are more likely to place a lower value on the total potential income from the use of new knowledge than its creators. This is due to the greater uncertainty buyers may have over the market demand for goods and services incorporating the new knowledge than its creators, even when possible dissipation of knowledge through copying is prohibited by patent. Hence there hardly exists a separate market for such a 'product'.

But to make investment in R&D worthwhile, total costs, including direct spending and the interest or opportunity cost of borrowed funds, have to be recovered over time from the sale of goods and services embodying new knowledge. Such recovery of costs may be attempted by the firm solely through its parent and branch plants or jointly by licensing others to use the research knowledge (technology). In the latter case, the licensor loses part of the revenue it might have earned from its sole use of the technology, hence the need to charge the licensee a rental fee. This explains why technology tends to be rented rather than sold outright.

Just as renting a house is an attempt by the tenant to limit the possible loss in the capital value of the house, renting the use of technology may be perceived as an attempt by its users to avoid possible loss of capital value from an outright purchase. Indeed, production of goods and services with rented knowledge ceases when their users no longer find the market returns from its use to be worth the rental fees.[10] It appears, therefore, to be inaccurate to depict a firm's use of technology which it has developed as an internalization of the technology market, unless we want to equate the firm's action with 'internalization' of the house rental market when an owner occupies the house.

In summary, several of the distinctive characteristics often associated with MNCs, including large scale, high R&D expenditures, sale of 'technology-intensive' (read, high-quality) and differentiated products, and high management and marketing skills may equally well be identified with UNCs or single-country firms. Their differences may be a matter of degree, not of a kind. In a sense, MNCs are merely better at doing on a larger scale what most multi-plant UNCs do. And their better performance has to be traced mainly to the organizational skills of their entrepreneur–managerial group, the factor which, as Coase (1937) also argues, imposes the optimal limit on the size of a firm.

Reconciling competing theories of the MNC

Existing theories of the multinational corporation are really attempts to explain foreign direct investment (FDI) rather than descriptions of an institutional arrangement, a firm. Thus, these theories present an 'outside', instead of an 'inside', view of the MNC.[11] A group of these theories, conceived within the neoclassical theory of international trade, explains the foreign production activities of the MNC as one of the forms in which the assumption of perfect competition employed in neoclassical economics is violated (e.g. Grosse 1985). If markets were perfectly competitive, it is argued, production would take place within UNCs, whose output would then be traded between countries, mainly on the basis of their relative factor abundance. MNCs are thus seen as replacing international trade in final goods and services with trade in inputs, including skilled labour, technology, and intermediate goods, often in response to trade-distorting tariffs and subsidies in host countries.

Another group of 'outside-the-firm' theories about the MNC are those within the industrial organization framework.[12] These identify MNCs as large monopolistic firms which attempt to exploit their firm-specific advantages, typically acquired through R&D, in the form of management and marketing skills, high technology-embodied or differentiated products, etc., in foreign countries through direct investment. According to this view, MNCs are rent-seekers for their monopolized assets. Several of their activities are also regarded as market-closing or competition-eliminating against other firms within a global economy.[13] On the basis of neoclassical welfare economics, whose normative standards are built upon the assumption of perfectly competitive markets, activities of MNCs are frequently regarded as welfare-reducing. Thus, it is legitimate for governments to intervene in markets in which MNCs operate even on a collaborative scale to improve welfare in the world.

The inadequacies of the above forms of theorizing on MNCs and the misleading policy prescriptions they have tended to generate have been pointed out by those who take an 'inside-the-firm' view of MNCs, in the form of the 'internalization theory of FDI' (e.g. Dunning and Rugman 1985; Rugman 1981, 1986).[14] This view is an application of Coase's description of the firm as an institution that seeks to reduce the transactions costs, hence economic inefficiencies, associated with using arm's-length markets by conducting desired transactions within the firm. Among important early contributors to its development are McManus (1972), Buckley and Casson (1976), Dunning (1977), and Magee (1977), but Rugman (1980, 1981, 1986) has been its most consistent proponent, arguing that 'existing theories of FDI are really subcases of the theory of internalization' (Rugman 1980: 370).[15] This approach supersedes similar attempts to integrate trade or location theory and industrial organization theories of the firm into an eclectic theory of FDI by Dunning (1977).[16]

The transactions costs internalized by MNCs, according to this theory, include recontracting for input supplies, transportation or co-ordination costs in dealing with foreign suppliers or sellers of the firm's products, tariffs and discriminatory quotas imposed by foreign governments, or the high cost of protecting proprietory knowledge abroad. The 'internal' creation and use of new knowledge (technology) by such firms at home and abroad are also explained in terms of market 'imperfections' or failure. That is, the absence of an open market for the sale of technology. In contrast with the industrial organization view of FDI, the internalization approach thus explains the activities of MNCs mainly in terms of efficiency-seeking, and hence welfare-improving behaviour. This is reckoned by their achievement of greater production and sales than otherwise would have occurred.

However, the argument of internalization theory can be made more consistent with reality – that is, with conditions of the marketplace – and with its advocates' goal of promoting more informed policies towards MNCs (e.g. Dunning and Rugman 1985). To achieve this, internalization theory has to be liberated from the constraining definition of competition in neoclassical economics in terms of a market structure rather a process of exchange. According to the neoclassical definition, perfect competition exists when no firm acts competitively by varying the price or quality of its goods and services. That is, firms do not compete in a perfectly competitive market structure! McNulty (1968: 641) makes the point succinctly:[17]

it is one of the great paradoxes of economic science that every *act* of competition on the part of a businessman is evidence, in economic theory, of some degree of monopoly power, while the concepts of monopoly and perfect competition have this important feature: both are situations in which the possibility of any competitive behaviour has been ruled out by definition.

The modern neoclassical definition of competition is a late nineteenth and early twentieth century distortion of the classical view of competition, as well as the ordinary meaning of the verb 'to compete', that is, a description of a market process.[18] It has led to the inaccurate view that activities of MNCs designed to compete more effectively with their rivals is evidence of insufficient competition in the marketplace.

But if rivalrous behaviour, the meaning classical and some early neoclassical economists attributed to 'competition', were adopted, internalization theory of FDI would not have to claim the existence of market imperfections in order to explain the activities of MNCs. The costliness, hence the economic inefficiencies, of some arm's-length transactions may suffice. As Alfred Marshall (1964: 4) explained, 'The strict meaning of competition seems to be the racing of one person against another, with special reference to bidding for the sale or purchase of anything.' He also considered the structure of industry – which includes the size and number of firms – secondary to the meaning of competition, arguing: 'This kind of racing is no doubt both more intense and more widely extended than it used to be: but it is only secondary, and one might say, an accidental consequence from the fundamental characteristics of modern industrial life.'[19] It surely cannot be argued that until the 1950s when there was little foreign direct investment around the world, particularly in manufacturing enterprises, factor or product markets were 'perfect', hence there was no incentive for the development of MNCs.

Furthermore, adoption of a more realistic view of the incentives for the emergence of MNCs would help to resolve the ambivalence some proponents of the internalization theory of FDI appear to have over whether the activities of MNCs are efficiency- and/or welfare-improving. The case can be made more easily against direct intervention in the operations of MNCs by governments, motivated perhaps by the noble intent of creating a 'more competitive' market structure as postulated in neoclassical welfare economics.

For example, Willmore (1976: 513) argues that 'A case might be made for a selective restriction of direct investment flows on the grounds that the presence of foreign subsidiaries increases the extent of monopoly power and lessens competition in local industries.' The error of this policy prescription is easier to recognize when competition is understood to mean rivalry. Rivalry is not reduced by the large size of some firms, and competition is better promoted by the absence of restraints on entry into industries.

The definition of competition as rivalrous behaviour, along with a clearer appreciation of the arguments of classical and early neoclassical economists based on 'free competition' or 'free enterprise', may also help in making another point. That is, the main source of monopoly power of firms, UNCs or MNCs, is their protection from competition by governments, in the form of tariffs, subsidies, or quotas. John S. Mill (1965: 3: 927–8) made this point very well:

> Governments . . . are often chargeable with having attempted, too successfully, to make things dear, than having aimed by wrong means at making them cheap. The usual instrument for producing artificial dearness is monopoly . . . . The mere exclusion of foreigners, from a branch of industry open to the free competition of every native, has been known . . . to render that branch a conspicuous exception to the general industrial energy of the country.

Even where such monopolies develop 'naturally', for example, from the economies of scale within an industry, their monopoly control over the goods and services they sell cannot endure for long without government protection. The remedy to any harmful monopolistic behaviour by MNCs must thus be found in the abandonment of government policies that protect the firms from competition from other firms, both local and foreign, rather than the harassment of MNCs directly.

On the other hand, one must also appreciate that not all exercise of monopoly power is harmful to a community's well-being. For example, a firm's exclusive ownership of knowledge (technology) may be regarded as a monopoly asset. It is also because of its social usefulness that other users are willing to pay rental fees for such knowledge. But the investment to create such an asset might not have been made were it not possible for the owner to charge 'monopoly rents' for its use. And community welfare might have been less without the creation and use of such a monopoly asset.

Understanding the beneficience of voluntary and free-market processes, whether we call them monopolistic or competitive, may enable us to appreciate Adam Smith's warning about the temptation of legislators to intervene directly in the marketplace:

> The statesman, who should attempt to direct private people in what manner they ought to employ their capital, would not only load himself with a most unnecessary attention, but assume an authority which could safely be entrusted, not only to no single person but to no council or senate whatever, and which would no-where be so dangerous as

in the hands of a man who had folly and presumption enough to fancy himself fit to exercise it.

(Smith 1976: 1: 478)

Smith did not rely on the assumption of (atomistic) perfect competition to argue the case for non-interventionist policies the way neoclassical welfare economics suggests. Rather, he based his arguments on the limitations of the human mind, the modern equivalent of which is 'bounded rationality'. In the absence of market intervention in the form of restraints or subsidies, Smith argued:

The sovereign is completely discharged from a duty, in the attempting to perform which he must always be exposed to innumerable delusions, and for the proper performance of which no human wisdom or knowledge could ever be sufficient; the duty of superintending the industry of private people, and of directing it towards the employment most suitable to the interest of the society.

(Smith 1976: 2: 208)

And there is plenty of evidence to confirm Smith's views on government direct intervention to regulate private enterprise.

In conclusion, we may describe the multinational corporation as a firm organized in pursuit of profits which, like many other large, modern corporations, has grown from its success. It is operated by an entrepreneur–managerial group whose rewards are linked with the fortunes of the firm. Like other multi-plant, but uninational firms, it gets around some of the transactions costs associated with using arm's-length markets by organizing several activities on an internal, contractual basis, including production, sales and purchases in more than one country. Among the important organizational decisions taken by the entrepreneurial group within the firm are: which and how much research and development expenditures to incur, in which regions to locate subsidiary plants, and the degree of autonomy to grant plant managers in their production and marketing activities in order to maximize total profits.

Chapter three

The firm in economic development

In Chapter 2 I emphasized the point that uninational and multinational corporations are very similar institutions, and that differences between them are a matter of degree, not of a kind. I take the same position here in discussing the role of MNCs in the economic development process of host countries. The distinguishing factor between the firms is the degree to which one type may excel over the other with respect to some specific characteristics conducive to economic development.

Before assessing the roles of UNCs and MNCs, it may be useful to distinguish between the concepts of economic growth and development. Economic growth is usually defined as the increase in the stock of economic assets, including consumption goods and services, producers' goods, and skills or non-human capital over a given period of time. Growth is thus measured as change in per capita gross domestic (or national) product, usually over one year. Economic development, on the other hand, is defined to include other characteristics besides per capita income growth. Thus economic development is said to have occurred when per capita income has been rising in addition to improvements in the distribution of income, a greater proportion of the population having gained more access to schools, hospitals, means of communication and transportation over time, and the techniques of production and the quality of life in general have improved.[1]

Some analysts would also include greater participation in political decision-making by the majority of the population among the indicators of development. This is an attempt to include in the definition of development aspects of the human existence besides those considered economic. By this criterion societies ruled by dictatorships, civilian or military, are judged as less developed than those governed by democracies. Whatever the merits of this criterion in judging the level of development, it is one which is quite marginal in assessing the role of firms in the process of development.

The focus on equity in the distribution of economic assets may cause some to claim the occurrence of development while per capita income is stagnant. Thus, through the redistribution activities of government, access to improved medical facilities, schools, recreational activities, and modern means of transportation and communication could be provided as public goods and paid for mainly through taxes. However, such a conclusion carries with it some dangers: the disincentive effects of the redistribution activities of government may result sooner or later in negative growth of aggregate national income. Such government activities then constitute a redistribution of poverty rather than wealth. The development experiences of LDCs such as Cuba, Ghana, Jamaica, Sri Lanka, and Tanzania, particularly since the 1960s, illustrate this process.[2]

The focus on equity in the definition of development may lead to another conclusion. A country experiencing a healthy economic growth of, say, 5 per cent annual per capita income growth or more, may yet be regarded as not experiencing development if most of the economic assets are owned by a small proportion of the population, and the quality of life for the majority does not improve. Clower *et al.* (1966), for example, judge the development record of Liberia on this basis. The development experiences of Brazil and Mexico, especially during the 1970s, have been described in similar terms (see, for example, Meier 1989: 21–5). But the danger with concentrating on equity in the definition of development is that real improvements in the absolute standard of living for the poor can seriously be underplayed while increases in absolute poverty along with greater equality may escape recognition.[3]

From the above distinction between growth and development, we can anticipate that the contributions of firms would directly affect economic growth more than economic development, however the latter concept is defined. Firms are established by entrepreneurs primarily because of the profits (residual incomes) they expect to earn from the enterprises in which they may be engaged. Equity in the distribution of the gains from such enterprises are not their prime concern. Rather they are concerned with whether the recipients of incomes contribute at least equivalent amounts to the total revenue of the firms.

In any case, equity is a concept subject to several interpretations, some not very helpful in a scientific discussion. If we mean by equity, giving to people what they deserve, then it is hard not to accept market-determined prices as equitable. Such prices result from the interplay of at least two subjective valuations, those of the buyer and seller. Unless force is applied, the transaction cannot be completed without both parties accepting a final (market) price. By this interpretation, firms paying wages, interest, rent, and prices of other inputs their owners freely chose to accept owe no other duty towards equity.

Firms are also not primarily concerned with the provision of other means for improving the quality of life for the majority of a population, including education, health, transport, and communication facilities for a community. Firms may invest in the creation of such facilities if by such expenditures their profits are increased, thus fulfilling implicitly the mandate of those with whose capital they are in business.

The contributions of firms towards economic growth and development are thus to be assessed in respect of their creation of demand for the services of a country's land, labour, and capital to be employed in the creation of new wealth or value added. Because of the payments received from the use of these productive assets, their owners may also strive to create more of them. Owners of uncultivated plots of land sell or rent more of them when demand increases, more people invest in the acquisition of skills because of higher wages, and owners of wealth save and purchase more financial assets at the inducement of higher interest or dividend payments. Without the demand by firms for such factors, fewer quantities would be created in an economy as everyone strives to be self-sufficient but ends up being less efficient in most things. Through the greater acquisition of such assets because of their demand by firms, an economy experiences more growth.

Finally, firms contribute to economic growth by directly creating or transforming raw materials into more useful forms or services as demanded by consumers. It is in identifying such consumer needs that entrepreneurs are said to be engaged in the process of discovering consumers' preferences (Kirzner 1973). Firms most successful in satisfying such preferences make the most profits while those that satisfy them the least make losses. It is also an illustration of how the self-interested pursuit of some individuals (entrepreneurs) confers benefits on numerous others, as so well explained by Adam Smith (1976: 1: 18, quoted in Chapter 2).

Given the incentive for making profits or losses in the marketplace, firms choose their factor combinations on the basis of their contributions to total revenue (marginal revenue productivity) relative to the rewards (prices) they command. In a system of 'perfect liberty' or 'free enterprise', as Adam Smith and other classical economists argued (not 'perfect competition'), factor rewards would be determined solely by the interaction of market supply and demand. Factors in plentiful supply relative to demand would command lower prices and more of them would also be hired for production. On the other hand, factors in less plentiful supply relative to demand command higher prices. In a world of less free enterprise, especially where governments set some factor rewards, firms still attempt to equate factor prices to the marginal revenue productivity of factors. But the quantities hired no longer reflect their relative physical abundance, thus creating unemployment for some factors whose marginal revenue productivities fall below the rewards they demand or are mandated by government policy.

Government policies thus play a crucial role in economic growth and development as these affect firms' demand for the economic assets of households. By enabling factor rewards to reflect their opportunity costs in the economy, government policies make possible greater production at the most efficient costs. But by setting factor prices at variance with their opportunity costs, government policies make production costs rise above their free-market levels and reduce the growth of total output in the economy. Furthermore, such policies cause some resources to be unemployed, which increases the inequality of income distribution.

For example, a minimum-wage policy keeps some unskilled workers employed at higher incomes than they otherwise would have earned, but it also locks out many such potential workers from being employed in the formal sector as firms economize on the use of such labour and substitute other factors, particularly machinery, in their place. Some of those potential workers may also have to settle for much lower-paying, informal sector jobs than they would have got in the absence of the mandated minimum wage. The use of more machinery may also increase the demand for more skilled personnel in substitution for unskilled labour.

A similar consequence results from the setting of interest rates below market-clearing levels by the government.[4] It may be anticipated that such low interest rates would enable more investors to borrow cheaply to buy raw materials and equipment, and hire the services of land and labour. Some firms may be able to do so, but many others would not find enough funds to borrow since lower, non-equilibrium interest rates discourage savings, particularly in the formal credit market. Some investors may have to borrow in the informal capital market at rates several times the government-mandated rate of interest. The low interest policy may thus reduce the interest income of some savers in the formal credit market and enrich lenders in the informal market, worsening the distribution of (interest) income from capital. Besides, if total savings fall as a result of the low-interest policy, total investment and economic growth also fall.

Distinguishing the contributions of multinational corporations

In what sense then may the contributions of MNCs be distinguished from those of local firms? This can be done by estimating the degree to which they contribute to economic growth through their production activities. The scale of enterprise assumes a major significance in this regard. If MNCs operate on a larger scale than UNCs, this may imply that they create a greater incentive for the acquisition of productive assets by households, particularly savings and skills, although their impact on savings may be rather indirect.[5] The larger scale of production may also imply a greater demand for the services of land. Considered from another angle, a larger scale may translate into a larger contribution per establishment to dividends, interest, rental, and wage income streams for the economy.

However, it is important to qualify the use of differences in scale as an indicator of the relative contributions of firms to economic growth and development. The index is useful when considering private-sector firms whose operations are not subsidized by the state. In the absence of subsidies, firms expand their production only because they are efficient enough to operate on a larger scale. Scale may thus serve as proxy for the relative technical or managerial as well as marketing efficiency of firms. But large-scale production sustained by subsidies, as is the case with many state enterprises, mostly constitutes a waste of economic resources and a source of growth retardation. The losses incurred by such enterprises (for which they require subsidies to maintain production) indicate the extent to which their use of resources generates less new wealth (value added) than otherwise could have been obtained.

An alternative index of the firm's relative contribution to economic growth may be total profits.[6] Profits summarize the economic efficiency of firms in being able to satisfy the preferences of the marketplace and rewarding productive factors, including interest-earning capital, labour (skilled and unskilled), and land in the process. Profits also indicate the firm's potential for expansion from own savings or the ability to attract more equity capital.

Another index for assessing the relative contributions of firms (MNCs or UNCs) may be their responsiveness to economic shocks or elasticities of substitution. A slower response to changing economic conditions (whether in interests, rental cost of land or equipment, or in wages) may cause a firm to operate at higher average costs than if the firm were able to adjust input combinations faster. Such slower response may also mean a limited ability to expand production in response to a fall in input costs, hence a smaller contribution to economic growth. A slower responsiveness may also mean a lesser contribution to development (in terms of relative income distribution), by its inhibition of greater use of factors whose relative costs have decreased.

Finally, the relative contributions of MNCs to economic development may be assessed from the differences in the quality of goods and services they produce, compared with those of their local counterparts. If we accept contributions to the quality of life in the definition of development, then this criterion is justified. However, its use must be tied to acceptance of consumers' preferences as indicators of their well-being. Such a framework prevents the analysis from being distracted by paternalistic arguments related to the definition of 'appropriate' products, as in, for example, Stewart (1977), Lall and Streeten (1977), and James (1982).[7]

22

However, it may be difficult to account adequately for differences in the quality of products between groups of firms from published statistics. On the presumption that appreciation of superior quality in the marketplace is revealed in higher profits, such an assessment may be approximated by the differences in total profits. Alternatively, differences in scale or value added among firms may serve the same purpose, on the somewhat tenuous premise that firms producing better-quality products (in the judgement of consumers) attract a higher volume of sales within the same industry.

However, we must bear in mind that, whatever conclusions we derive from the above method of assessing the contributions of firms to economic growth and development, the conclusions are only relative. Such conclusions do not negate the fact that both types of firms may have contributed positively to economic growth and development by hiring local factors and transforming local materials into higher stages of utility generation. Without the activities of either group of firms, total wealth creation and rewards to local factors (hence national income) would have been smaller. It is hard to conceive of foreign direct investment merely substituting for local investment, both private and public. Even where local firms are bought by foreign firms, their purchase prices (capital values) constitute potential investment funds which could be employed elsewhere in the economy.

The traditional assessment of MNCs

The emphasis of the above approach to assessing the contributions MNCs make to economic growth and development in host countries differs from that often encountered in the literature. The latter places more emphasis on the contributions of MNCs to the stock of capital, technology (embodied in equipment, products, marketing, and management skills), access to foreign markets (hence increased earnings of foreign exchange), and increases to government tax revenue. This approach follows mainly the work of MacDougall (1960).[8] Notable exceptions include, Vernon (1972, 1975), Reuber (1973), Johnson (1975), and Lal (1975).

For most LDCs, the traditional approach seems quite sensible. Because of low incomes and poorly developed capital markets, financial capital accumulation is rather limited in these countries. The problem of capital formation is also worsened where governments adopt low, regulated interest rate policy in the mistaken belief that it will promote faster economic growth through increased investment. Foreign investment with funds acquired abroad thus partly relieves the shortage of financial capital, and makes greater production possible. Such additions of foreign capital may also relieve pressure on the rate of interest charged in the informal money and capital markets.

Less-developed countries are also technology poor. This poverty partly accounts for their lower levels of production or efficiency in the transformation of materials into more useful (greater utility-generating) stages. And there is much less investment in new technology creation both by firms and governments of these countries, as compared with such investment in the more-developed countries (MDCs). But the development of new technology – products, production methods, marketing techniques as well as management – is one of the major strengths of MNCs. Indeed, it is very much the possession of some technological advantage over their competitors at home (UNCs) that enables MNCs to overcome early diminishing returns to scale and expand their operations. It is also such technological advantage that enables them to engage in production abroad and make profits in the unfamiliar environment of different laws, customs, languages, work habits, and sometimes climate. Their technological advantage is thus a counter to their relative disadvantage compared with their local counterparts in dealing with the host environment. The introduction of new technology by MNCs may thus contribute significantly to the growth potential of host countries.

Beyond the direct benefits the introduction of these productive assets by MNCs may contribute to host countries, the traditional aproach also emphasizes indirect benefits from the operations of these firms. Local enterprises are expected to imitate the quality of new products, marketing and management techniques, and also benefit from hiring some of the skilled personnel trained by MNCs. Such positive influences on domestic firms are sometimes assessed to be even more significant for the host countries since MNCs cannot charge for them. They are regarded as positive 'externalities' to host countries.

The emphasis on increased foreign exchange earning capacity made possible by the production activities of MNCs is based partly on the argument that MNCs have a better knowledge of world demand conditions, particularly in their home (source) countries for products manufactured in the host countries. Therefore, they are expected to be better at marketing them abroad.

A related argument is that foreign firms tend to be granted preferential treatment with respect to import duties levied by their home governments. Where such treatment exists, MNCs are able to export more than their local competitors in LDCs.[9] For the LDC economy, total exports increase, and the receipts from such sales tend to be considered additions to the stock of foreign exchange earned by the host country. For many development analysts and LDC governments who regard foreign-exchange scarcity as one of the significant constraints on their ability to develop, the greater capacity to export, made possible by the activities of MNCs, is thus regarded as an important contribution to economic growth and development.

The foreign-exchange scarcity argument for explaining the difficulty of economic development has been formalized into the so-called two-gap hypothesis (see, for example, Chenery and Strout 1966). But as has been pointed out (e.g. Bruton 1969; Blomqvist 1976), it is largely a misleading argument. In a fully flexible exchange regime, there is no meaningful way of describing a foreign-exchange shortage. The market price of foreign currency equates the quantities of foreign exchange willingly demanded and supplied. Thus, the foreign-exchange shortage argument is but an example of how some analysts forsake application of valid economic principles to the development problems of LDCs.[10]

Finally, taxes paid by MNCs as well as other foreign firms are considered an important contribution to the development potential of host countries. Meier (1984: 324), for example, observes that:

> For many countries, taxes on foreign profits or royalties from concession agreements constitute a large proportion of total government revenue. . . . The fiscal benefit derived from foreign investment is evident from the fact that the share of government revenue in the national product of countries that have received substantial foreign investment is considerably higher than in most of the other low-income countries.

And since governments play a significant role in the process of wealth and income redistribution, considered a significant aspect of development, such contributions to government revenue by MNCs are considered very important. Moreover, such taxes are considered as contributions over and above payments already made to local factors of production. In other words, they ensure that more of the gross value added in production is acquired by residents (including the government) of the host country than otherwise would have been the case.

However, by reducing the after-tax rate of return or profits for MNCs, the taxes may cause the total amount of capital invested to be smaller than otherwise. Whether the additional incomes that domestic factors could have earned from the greater capital investment would have exceeded the profit taxes collected by government depends on a complex set of factors. They include the income (dividend) elasticity of supply of capital (savings), the income elasticity of supply of domestic factors, and the price elasticity of demand for the firms' product(s). Furthermore, it is an empirical question whether government spending of the revenue from profit taxes promotes more economic development than the additional private spending that would have occurred in the absence of profit taxes. Thus, it is possible to overestimate the positive contributions of government tax revenues from the profits of MNCs.

Pitted against the above positive assessments of the contributions of

MNCs to the economic growth and development of host countries are their alleged contributions to balance of payments difficulties, a drain on investment capital, introduction of inappropriate products and techniques, and the loss of national sovereignty. Significant contributors to this literature include Baran and Sweezy (1966), Streeten (1972), Evans (1972), Sunkel (1972), Streeten and Lall (1973), Barnet and Muller (1974), and Hymer (1979).[11]

The balance of payments difficulties are alleged to arise from remittances of MNCs to pay dividends to shareholders and royalties or rents to parent companies for the use of technology. When such external flow of remittances exceeds incoming investment funds, some analysts consider the foreign payments to be a source of balance of payments difficulties for host countries (see, for example, Hood and Young 1979, chapter 5; Streeten and Lall 1973). Such remittances are also sometimes regarded as a drain on the host country's potential growth-promoting capital, a 'decapitalization effect' as it has been called (e.g. Bornschier 1980).[12]

In contrast to the positive assessment of MNCs on the basis of taxes and royalties they pay to host governments, some analysts also charge that MNCs (illegally) extract huge sums of funds from LDCs through transfer pricing. They are alleged to inflate the value of imports (materials, equipment, and machinery as well as technology) and undervalue their exports, and are thus able to more than offset the amounts they pay as taxes (see, for example, Robbins and Stobaugh 1973; Vaitsos 1974; Natke 1985).[13] According to this argument, transfer pricing by MNCs is just another mechanism through which foreign firms impoverish LDCs to the advantage of MDCs.

A related concern over the balance of payments effects of production by MNCs is the alleged worsening of host LDCs' commodity terms of trade. It is claimed that increased production of exportable commodities by MNCs (sometimes) reduces their exchange values relative to the value of imports. This argument is buttressed by the fact that the world price elasticity of demand for most major exports from LDCs is usually less than unity. It is, therefore, suggested that worsening terms of trade from increased exports reduce the income (well-being) of affected LDCs.[14]

Critics of MNCs also argue that these firms retard economic growth and development of LDCs by their choice of production techniques alleged to be too capital-intensive for the relatively labour-abundant LDCs. Besides, such techniques distort the distribution of value added in favour of foreign factors (equipment, machinery, and skills) and against local factors in LDCs. The firms are also accused of introducing products which cater mainly to the tastes of a rich minority while ignoring the needs of the poor majority. These firms thus fail to increase the general welfare of the population, according to this argument.[15]

Finally, some critics allege that, because of their relative size, MNCs are able to hold LDC governments to political ransom by threatening to close plants and cause significant unemployment. They are also accused of corrupting government officials to act according to the firms' profit interests, or inviting retribution from powerful home governments (e.g. the US) on their behalf in times of dispute with host governments.[16] The overthrow and assassination of President Allende of Chile in 1973 is often cited as an example of the retribution that MNCs (here IT&T) can bring upon a hostile LDC government.

Reconciling the competing assessments

The arguments of both the critics of MNCs and those who attribute to them mainly positive contributions to the economic growth of LDCs are both partially correct. The problem with either approach appears to be that of overstatement. Concentrating on assessing the contributions of MNCs and other foreign firms in terms of their creation of wealth for domestic factors avoids this problem.

Investment by foreign firms increases the demand for the stock of a nation's capital, labour, and land, hence increasing the national income of host countries from the earnings of interest, dividends, wage, and rental incomes. This method of assessment may also help towards greater appreciation of the need for foreign firms to pay factors owned by foreigners, including capital (dividends), technology (rents or royalties), and management (professional salaries). It may also help to make the argument that whatever amounts of annual profit a foreign firm remits, they cannot exhaust the wealth or gross value added produced by the firm over a given period of time. Therefore, such remittances can hardly be a drain on the host country's source of investment capital. Similarly, transfer pricing as a means of repatriating profits (if they exist) may be recognized as remittances not of domestic factor incomes but of the firm.[17] The country's own investment capital can only come from savings out of incomes earned by local factors of production.

The fallacy of attributing balance of payments difficulties to such remittances may also be more easily recognized within this framework. The incomes of foreign factors working in the host country, which properly must to be regarded as imports, have to be paid. Besides the fixity of exchange rates that creates the notion of foreign-exchange shortage, the country experiences a balance of payments problem because it does not export enough (including certificates of indebtedness or IOUs) to pay for its imports of foreign factors. Moreover, such imports could have been undertaken by local firms, as in cases where they produce under licence.

The focus of the factor incomes approach adopted in this chapter may also be helpful in recognizing the misleading nature of the declining terms of trade argument against MNCs. Factor owners will not persist in any economic activities for long unless they benefit from doing so. Therefore, a fall in export prices which does not reduce the incomes of producers should be of little concern to anyone else. Even if export prices should fall sufficiently for producers' incomes to decline, we can expect that they would either curtail their production or change activities. Such reaction on the part of producers is what efficiency in the allocation of resources in an economy warrants. Rather than being detrimental to economic growth, it promotes growth.

One may concede that the attempt by all foreign firms to repatriate their capital at the same time could create temporary balance of payments difficulties for the host country. But even that situation has to be evaluated within its proper context. It represents an increase in the demand by local entrepreneurs or the government to purchase foreign-owned assets. Without such demand, the market value of such firms would be reduced to near zero or significantly enough for there to be hardly any noticeable balance of payments difficulties from their desire to repatriate funds. Indeed, in a flexible exchange rate regime, the attempt to repatriate large sums of capital would create a loss for fund remitters. Thus, if capital repatriation appears to create balance of payments difficulties, such difficulties must be recognized as having been produced simultaneously by an increased demand for foreign-owned assets (imports) by nationals.

The factor incomes approach to the assessment of the impact of MNCs also helps a more informed discussion of issues, including the question of sovereignty, often relegated to the realm of socio-political debate. For example, the threat of retribution by a foreign power may enable MNCs to be left alone to pursue greater wealth creation for nationals of a host country (albeit as a by-product of the firms' profit-seeking interest). The additional wealth so created has to be contrasted with the diminution of national pride – mainly felt or espoused by leaders of the host government.

Indeed, it appears that governments complain about their loss of sovereignty from the presence of MNCs when they estimate that the anger of the nationals who would be thrown out of work if the MNCs left may exceed their feelings of national pride from learning why the government forced their exit. Without such an assessment, the possibility of plant closures would be of little concern to host governments in their dealings with MNCs. The popularity of the government might even be bolstered by such actions, which may be perceived as standing up to a foreign power![18]

Furthermore, it should be possible for a government to publicize the misdeeds of MNCs and for citizens to voluntarily boycott their products or withhold sale of economic resources to them as an indication of their displeasure or national pride, if they feel sufficiently aggrieved. It would be difficult for a foreign (home) government to intervene in such a situation.

If MNCs pay bribes to officials of host governments, they would likely not be at the expense of local factor incomes, but probably that of government tax revenue or out of the firm's current profits. The former entails a redistribution of wealth from the public to private domain within the nation, while the latter is an addition to national wealth. However, bribes would be paid out of the firm's profits typically in anticipation of greater future production and profits – a kind of business expense. Within the above framework of evaluation, the concern should be whether the bribes enable greater wealth creation for domestic factors than not.

Firms typically do not go about giving out part of their investment capital (often borrowed funds) to government officials unless it enables them to evade restrictions on their avenues for profits. The prevalence of business bribery and corruption may thus reflect the existence of economically inefficient regulations. If so, they signal the need to examine the economic usefulness of regulations which MNCs and other firms avoid by bribing government officials.

On the other hand, the prevalence of bribery and corruption may indicate a high degree of moral decay within the host government, requiring self-cleansing rather than blame on foreign and other firms for having yielded to the demands for bribes. Either way the activities of MNCs would seem to signal areas of remedial action for host governments to facilitate greater efficient economic growth and development.

We can summarize the role of MNCs in economic growth and development as follows. Like any other firm, the MNCs contribute to economic growth and development by creating demand for productive factors of host countries, and transforming materials into more useful (utility-generating) forms. Their payment of income to factor owners causes more of the economic assets whose accumulation is identified with economic growth and development to be created by households. In the absence of factor price distortions imposed by government policies, more of the relatively abundant (and cheaper) economic assets are also employed by firms, thus promoting equalization of factor incomes. The drive to make more profits also leads MNCs (as well as other firms) to develop higher quality products as well as management and marketing techniques that enhance the general quality of life within host countries. To the extent that local firms are able to imitate those activities of MNCs which are considered superior, the population of the host country gains in improved standard of living as well.

It is important to compare MNCs and local firms in the same product categories when assessing their relative contributions to an economy. That makes it easier to place their activities in a clearer perspective, particularly regarding those which some would consider as the costs of FDI, including importation of raw materials, equipment, and machinery, hiring of foreign skilled (professional) personnel, choice of techniques, over- and under-invoicing of imports and exports, respectively, and the payment of dividends to shareholders. Finally, one must assign correctly ownership claims to economic assets in order to avoid the misleading arguments which attribute balance of payments difficulties to the income repatriation of MNCs.

Chapter four

The technology of MNCs and economic development

As discussed in Chapter 3, one of the major contributions MNCs make to the economic growth and development process of host countries, particularly in LDCs, is the introduction of new technology – improved products and techniques of organizing firms, including production and marketing. Such new knowledge is created in anticipation of greater profits from the savings in costs or the increased production it makes possible. Although part of the benefits from the use of such knowledge is appropriated by MNCs in the form of royalties or licence fees, factor owners in the host country also gain from the increased income the greater production makes possible. Consumers also gain from the greater availability of improved products (goods and services) or their cheaper prices due to the use of new knowledge. Furthermore, to the extent local firms are able to imitate the technology of MNCs, indirect advantages are conferred on the population of the host country.

While most analysts grant the above contributions from MNCs to the development process, many also point to what they consider as adverse effects on host countries from the introduction of new technology. They argue that unless technology is appropriate to the resource endowments of a host country, its overall impact is detrimental to development. Such concern over the appropriateness of technology has spawned a vast literature. The purpose of this chapter is to explore this argument, in particular to discover the extent to which MNCs may be guilty of the charge of introducing inappropriate technology into host countries, or whether the charge makes sense at all. I conclude that much of the concern over technology choice in LDCs reflects the collectivist ideology of those who express it, rather than sound logic or the evidence of empirical studies.

Technology

Although most analysts are clear about the difference between technology and technique, the two concepts tend to be used interchangeably in many discussions. The practice sometimes can and does create analytical confusion. It may help the discussion, therefore, to restate the difference between the two concepts.

In its general conception, technology refers to knowledge – the art of doing things. In the realm of production, technology involves the art of combining inputs, including equipment, machinery, buildings, labour, raw materials, and skills to produce some given level of output. Technology also includes knowledge of the ability to rearrange inputs in response to variations in relative factor prices (elasticities of substitution), as well as changes in input mix along with the scale of production (scale elasticity of input mix). Thus, in terms of the familiar two-factor isocost–isoquant diagram, technology refers to a collection of points or techniques (capital–labour ratios) as well as the convexity of the line connecting these points (isoquant).

Furthermore, technology refers to the path of successive isoquants from the origin, indicating homotheticity or non-homotheticity of the underlying production function. Where successive isoquants lie on a straight line from the origin (homothetic function), input mix does not change with scale. For example, more capital is not preferred to labour at higher levels of production. But where the path of isoquants is not linear (non-homothetic production function), factor mix changes with scale. Finally, the description of technology includes methods of marketing and overall management of the enterprise. Clearly then, it is hard to describe or represent technology by a single index.[1] We can talk meaningfully only about the characteristics of technology.

However, not all those who discuss technology choice (especially writers dealing with LDCs) employ this broad characterization of technology. The notable exceptions include Bell (1972/73), Ishikawa (1972), Morawetz (1974), Leipziger (1976), Lipsey *et al.* (1978), Baranson (1978), and Pack (1984).[2] Many analysts use such narrow definitions of technology that they blur the distinction between technology and techniques. Examples include Cooper (1972/73), Streeten (1972), Ranis (1973), Pickett *et al.* (1974), Stewart (1977), Pack (1979), and Perkins (1983). The analysts who employ this narrow definition of technology do not dispute the validity of the broad definition of technology to include techniques. It is in their attempts to illustrate the choice of technology that they blur distinction between the two concepts.[3] When they use isoquant diagrams, these analysts depict technologies as points on a common industry isoquant, instead of identifying the points as techniques.[4] Some claim that the 'choice of technique is eliminated once the choice of product is made' (e.g. Stewart 1972: 109), and by the association of techniques with technologies (as in Pickett and Robson 1977 or Perkins 1983), they create the impression that judgement regarding the choice of technology can meaningfully be inferred from the characteristics of products.[5]

But unless technology is narrowly defined to mean the core process of a machinery (e.g. Pack 1984), and not different combinations of fixed assets with labour (and skills), this assertion would be misleading. Different qualities of a product may be manufactured with different combinations of factors (fixed assets, labour, and skills). And there is hardly any reason why determinants of Leibenstein's so-called 'x-efficiency' may not also improve the quality of products along with increases in their quantities.[6] As it turns out, the confusion of technology with technique by some analysts, partly accounts for their claim that foreign firms, particularly MNCs, employ 'inappropriate' technologies in host LDCs.

Definitions of appropriate technology

One definition of 'appropriate' technology employed in the literature is based on a country's relative physical factor abundance. Thus, for LDCs generally understood to be rich in labour but poor in capital (financial or physical) relative to the factor endowments of the more-developed, industrialized countries (MDCs), technology is considered appropriate if it uses relatively more labour than capital (machinery and equipment). But no absolute factor proportions are specified. Also, many do not admit any role for relative factor prices in determining which range of input combinations may be regarded as appropriate technology (e.g. Cooper 1972/73, 1982; Streeten 1972; Stewart 1977). But those who make reference to factor prices tend to focus on shadow prices instead. Thus, Morawetz (1974: 517), for example, suggests:[7]

> Appropriate technology may be defined as the set of techniques which make the optimum use of available resources in a given environment. For each process or project, it is the technology which maximizes social welfare if factors and products are *shadow priced* . . . . In general, technologies which are appropriate in labour surplus developing countries will use more unskilled labour than those appropriate in developed countries. (My emphasis)

Some other analysts merely subsume the factor-proportions criterion of appropriateness in their argument. For example, Perkins (1983) regards 'small scale techniques' as appropriate technology while large-scale, capital-intensive activities are considered inappropriate and wasteful of the country's (Tanzania) resources, without the standard of judgement being explicitly defined. Other characteristics often associated with 'appropriate' technology include little use of skilled labour (both managerial and production) and imported raw materials, and small scale. The other main definition of 'appropriate' technology is based on the profitability of embodied techniques. Technology is appropriate if it generates maximum profits.[8] This definition has the distinction of avoiding the factor-proportions bias necessarily entailed in the other, and allows relatively capital-, skill- and imported material-intensive techniques to be considered appropriate for LDCs. As Pack (1981: 32) observes, 'The appropriate technology . . . is not necessarily the most labour-intensive production method available if those that require even smaller investment per worker are less profitable.' And as Waldorf (n.d.: 101) reports from a study by Cooper *et al.*, 'One of the most interesting findings . . . is that the most labor-intensive technique never proves to be the minimum-cost technique' in Kenya, Tanzania, and Thailand. The profitability view of appropriateness is also consistent with Schumpeter's (1955: 13) observation that 'Every method of production in use at a given time bows to economic appropriateness', or else it is weeded out of the marketplace.[9] Of course, this argument assumes that the state does not subsidize prolonged use of unprofitable techniques.

Before considering the relevance of 'appropriate' technology for economic growth and development, I note some limitations of the definitions. First, there is a problem of identification. Since technology embodies a series of alternative techniques or combinations of factors, we typically can observe only a subset of techniques or characteristics of technology at a given point in time. Thus, even on the basis of factor proportions, it may be premature to judge a selection of techniques as indicating 'appropriate' technology. However, a set of techniques may be regarded as *more* appropriate than another within the same industry. Similarly, with regard to the profitability criterion, we can only designate a set of techniques as more appropriate than others if it yields the highest profits within the industry at a given point in time. But without knowing the amount of profits that possibly could be obtained from all other input combinations, we could not be sure we have found *the* appropriate technique, hence, technology.

There is also the difficulty of identifying technology which is universally appropriate, especially on the basis of the factor-proportions criterion. Firms can only choose from available techniques of production or invent new ones. Thus, although some past alternative methods of production may employ much more labour than capital, such techniques may no longer be available as they do not now meet the economic test of usefulness. For example, rowing boats may use more men per tonnage capacity than modern fuel-powered ships, but few of such means of transportation can readily be purchased for trans-ocean voyages, assuming one does not worry about the profitability of their use.[10] In other words, 'appropriate' technology, if defined over factor proportions, also changes over time.

Appropriate technology and economic development

The factor-proportions basis for defining 'appropriate' technology is founded on some developmental premises. Its proponents believe that production processes with the specified characteristics would generate a greater employment of labour, would be within the management capabilities of the people in the countries under consideration, and would confer the benefits of industrial production on a larger share of the population than production processes without them. They base these expectations on grounds of (physical) resource constraint and technical efficiency. Since LDCs are relatively poor in accumulated capital (financial or physical) as well as skills, production processes that economize on these factors, but utilize extensively the most abundant resource (unskilled labour), would generate the most growth in output. Production processes of this nature would also entail little payment of income to foreign factors, thus assuring a greater national income growth from production even within multinational enterprises.

Some proponents of the factor-proportions criterion of appropriateness also note that machine-paced processes typically produce superior quality products, and on a larger scale, compared with processes using mainly human hands.[11] But they are led by their concern for greater employment of labour to include production of inferior or second-rate quality products among the characteristics of technology appropriate for LDCs (e.g. Stewart 1972; 1974a and b; 1977).[12] They also point out that superior quality, capital-intensive products are typically more expensive, and are thus beyond the means of the poor, as compared with poorer quality alternatives (Stewart and James 1982). And since they consider catering for the needs of the poor in LDCs to be the main indicator of (successful) development, they regard the production of second-rate or cheaper quality, mainly hand-made (labour-intensive) products as the key to the attainment of that goal. These arguments are summarized in the succinct assertion by Pickett *et al.* (1974: 54), that 'labour-intensive processes being more organically grounded in developing countries should develop more rapidly and more wholesomely than the alternative in all directions'.

Some also argue that the additional investment in machinery and skills to manufacture improved products is mainly a waste of resources since such products contribute little additional biological benefits to consumers. Others, such as Stewart (1974b: 23), invoke a community standard for defining 'appropriate' products:

Inappropriate products are products with *excessive characteristics and standards* in relation to the needs and income levels of the country in question. Some characteristics may be excessive in the sense that they are neither useful or wanted . . . . Much more common are products whose characteristics are *excessive in relation to the poverty of society* but which are *nevertheless desired by those who consume them*. Cars, washing machines – almost any of the products of modern developed country consumer durable industries provide examples. They are not confined to consumer durables: the standard of durability and strength of textiles may be excessive; similarly of building materials and also other qualities such as heat and sound insulation. (My emphasis)

Note the collectivist ideology underlying this definition. According to this reasoning, wealth owners have no right to spend their wealth as they choose. Their choices have to be constrained by the level of poverty in a country (e.g. Stewart and James 1982: 13–14 and Stewart and James 1982: 225–55). Advocates of this view do not seem to recognize the fact that it is individuals who spend their incomes, not a community.[13]

However, arguments based on the collectivist definition of appropriate products are not as valid as their proponents may believe. First, the expectations of positive development impact from appropriate technology defined over physical characteristics may be disappointed unless firms employing them make profits. A private firm would have to close down if it persistently cannot pay its creditors, including banks, bondholders, and suppliers of materials, and pay attractive dividends to shareholders. If an enterprise fails, local labour bears part of the loss in terms of forgone employment opportunities. With zero income for a part of the labour force, the reduction in income inequality, which is an important goal in development as earlier defined, cannot be achieved.

On the other hand, techniques that are profitable but are capital goods-, imported materials- and skill-intensive, hold a greater prospect for continued employment of those local factors already hired. And from the profits more investments can be made, which help to generate greater employment of the country's most abundant physical resources. Thus, in terms of efficient and sustained long-term growth and development, only techniques that are profitable are appropriate.

Those who suggest reliance on shadow price calculations to promote greater employment of a country's physically (not economically) most abundant resources, in violation of the profitability calculations of private firms, thus appear to have missed the long-term growth implications of such a policy. Private firms may be induced to select unprofitable, labour-intensive techniques through wage subsidies, but funds for the subsidies would have to be appropriated through taxation of profitable enterprises as well as personal incomes. Borrowing from the country's central bank, which is, in effect, printing new money, typically creates inflation with little real income growth. Foreign loans are often project-specific, and can hardly be used for wage subsidies on a continuing basis. The policy thus amounts to channelling part of the investment capital (savings) in a country to sectors where they are less productive. The burden of taxation would thus retard investment in (more) profitable, but unsubsidized sectors. On the whole then, such a policy does not promote greater economic growth, it retards it.

A Keynesian argument may suggest that subsidizing greater employment of labour would raise aggregate demand and, through the multiplier process, promote economic growth. But that argument ignores the fact that production is made possible by capital accumulation or savings, and subsidization of employment in less profitable sectors reduces the amount of capital to be invested in more profitable alternatives.[14] Similarly, Griffin (1977: 68–9) also argues that production of cheap quality, 'employment-intensive' products would promote faster economic growth and development. However, the argument seems to ignore the fact that unless such products are in accord with the tastes and preferences of consumers, and yield profits, adopting policies to encourage their production will retard economic growth.

There are also serious difficulties in trying to implement correctly the subsidy–taxation policy to induce the choice of 'appropriate' techniques based on shadow prices.[15] First, shadow prices are imaginary numbers, incorporating the limited and static information available to some planner, policymaker, or analyst. Often the shadow prices are not industry- or sector-specific, which ideally must be the case.[16] For example, unskilled labour may not contribute the same (marginal) value of output in agriculture as it does in construction or manufacturing. This is why free-market wages of unskilled labour differ between industries. Given changing preferences of market participants, values obtained through market surveys may not be relevant when decisions based on them are implemented. Thus, inducing the choice of unprofitable techniques on the basis of shadow prices is just another form of economic distortion rather than a helpful correction. It is quicker, and far more efficient, to remove administrative prices (minimum wages, official exchange rates, and interest ceilings) than to try to reorient efficiently the selection of techniques of production through taxes and subsidies.

Textbook perfectly competitive markets do not exist in the real world. But that is not a valid reason for claiming that free, non-administered market prices are not 'right', and hence, that techniques selected on the basis of such prices are inappropriate.[17] Those who dispute this fact carry over the confused definition of competition in neoclassical economics (see Chapter 2) into policy prescription, and suggest that governments in LDCs get prices 'right' by setting them at levels that would compensate for the absence of perfectly competitive markets.

Note that my criticism of the shadow-price criterion for selecting techniques is not against the need to adjust market prices to reflect uncompensated negative or positive externalities which may arise because of difficulties in enforcing private property rights. My argument is against the imposition of third-party views of appropriateness on individual participants in the marketplace; goods and services bought and sold at free-market prices reveal the convergent preferences of both buyers and sellers. Buyers who find such prices to be above their (subjective) value of the items refuse to buy them. Those who buy them also try to ensure that their values are at least worth the income they give up (prices) for the last quantity bought. Sellers engage in a reverse calculation, trying to ensure that they obtain the highest possible income for their subjective value of resources they give up in the sale. Therefore, there is no valid basis for any third party (economist or politician) who is no part of the voluntary transaction, to impose their preferences on others by declaring the exchange values (prices) to be inappropriate.

The policy of prescribing 'appropriate' products, if implemented, would also reduce the well-being of most people in LDCs. It must be noted that what today are considered superior quality products may be tomorrow's second-rate items; and today's second-rate products, including 'semi-processed foodstuffs, coarse clothing, inexpensive crockery' (Griffin 1977: 68) were yesterday's superior products.[18] The question arises: Where in the product cycle – continuing discovery of improved products and subsequent obsolescence – are people of LDCs to be held back without lowering the average standard of living?

Moreover, only a few so-called superior products are completely absent from the consumption basket of most people in LDCs. This fact is amply demonstrated by the famous (or infamous) episode of poor mothers in these countries improperly feeding their infants with Nestlé's baby formula.[19] Rather, it is the mix of their consumption which may be different, reflecting their tastes, preferences, and levels of income and wealth. And those who cannot yet afford superior products aspire to consume them when their life's fortunes improve (income, transfer payments, or gifts of cash). Thus, in a survey of studies related to the composition of goods produced by MNCs in LDCs, Waldorf (n.d.: 108) finds that

> even a major redistribution of income from the rich to the poor would have only a minimal impact on temporal and intertemporal employment. That is, the implied shift from high-income to low-income consumption goods has a (surprisingly) negligible effect on overall employment.

To the extent that people's feelings of well-being are determined by the quality of goods and services they consume, prohibiting the consumption of superior quality products as public policy would hurt many more people than advocates of appropriate-products policy seem to appreciate. (At least from pictures, the people of China now appear much happier in their new clothes and jewellery, in restaurants, and in nightclubs, than they were under the 'appropriate' lifestyle prescribed by Mao Zedong before 1976.) Furthermore, there are people in LDCs with higher incomes than some in MDCs. Knowing that poorer people in MDCs have the freedom to spend their incomes as they please could not enhance their feeling of wellbeing.

In a mistaken attempt to link 'inappropriate' products with reduction in national welfare, Lall and Streeten (1977: 71) argue that

> [The] fulfillment of preferences expressed in the market is not the final criterion of welfare, certainly not in extremely poor countries, and that the use of scarce resources for the production of goods which are over-specified and within the reach of only a small elite, or, if bought by the poor, at the expense of more essential products, is not conducive to 'national welfare'.

Their argument ignores the fact that 'national welfare' can legitimately be derived only as the sum of individuals' welfare, as partly revealed in their purchasing habits in the marketplace. The argument also implies that the poor cannot tell what best suits their own feelings of well-being.

Of course, there may be resentment among the poor against the rich in the absence of an appropriate-products policy, but such resentment, aroused by envy, could also exist within income classes. Thus, although the policy might minimize its extent, it cannot eliminate it; envy is a pervasive human trait.[20] And in most communities, those who act out envious feelings through stealing or burglary are punished for violating the property rights of others.

Moreover, the attempt to eliminate resentment founded on envy of the more wealthy may rather reduce total income in the community, but removal of the resentment due to an appropriate-products policy would increase community income.[21] People can turn their envious feelings into a positive force for greater wealth creation or achievement – determination to work harder. Indeed, the degree to which people exert themselves to earn higher incomes is partly determined by the gap between their current status and the level they would like to attain, as well as the forms in which they can spend their incomes. Therefore, eliminating superior quality products from a country may dim the incentive for hard work, and hence retard economic growth.

The level of wealth in a country could also decline if the appropriate-products policy causes emigration of skilled personnel and capital exports by the wealthy. It is noteworthy that two Egyptian brothers were able to buy majority shares in Harrods of London in the early 1980s while the Egyptian government was looking for international aid. The greater freedom to earn and spend their income as they please in England as compared with Egypt must have something to do with their investment preference. Similarly, highly trained people have left countries influenced by advocates of appropriate technology and products, including India, Pakistan, and Tanzania, to work in countries that allow greater individual freedoms over the choice of techniques and commodities. Thus, it would be a more fruitful way of helping the poor if attention is directed towards, first, understanding the nature of obstacles to their ability to create more wealth, and then eliminating them, rather than implementing an appropriate-products policy which may leave the poor in greater poverty.

Another negative effect of an appropriate-product policy may be the reduction of income within the country's tourism industry. As is well known, tourists visit LDCs to enjoy sunny beaches and/or satisfy their curiosity, not to share in the poverty of those places.[22] This is why it has been profitable to operate high-quality hotels serving foreign meals and drinks to tourists at such locations. Therefore, unless implementation of the policy includes confining tourists to certain sectors of the country where items of their preferences are available (e.g. in China), the flow of tourists to LDCs may be reduced, retarding the growth of income in the country. On the other hand, the policy of limiting consumption of superior goods to tourists would also cause a feeling of resentment among the local population.

Finally, the appropriate-products policy has a strong potential for misallocating resources towards welfare-reducing activities. To be totally successful, the policy would require a considerable increase in expenditures on border patrols in order to stop the in-smuggling of foreign manufactured goods encouraged by the policy. Citizens arriving from abroad would attempt to bring prohibited products into the country, while professional smugglers would make enormous profits from trade in such items. It would be impossible to stop the smuggling completely. Thus, its main beneficiaries would be the smugglers, customs officials, and other security agents who would all share in the profits of such trade. Losers include all those who would have to purchase the items at higher prices, reflecting their scarcity premium.

Therefore, carefully considered, the belief that limiting the range of product quality in LDCs will improve the people's well-being is mistaken, although it may satisfy the collectivist or paternalistic taste of those who suggest the policy.[23] It is clear that the freedom of multinational corporations, as well as locally owned firms, to manufacture the types of products people in LDCs want contributes to raising their standard of living.

The characteristics of technology

The available evidence does not conclusively support the claim that foreign firms, including MNCs, choose more inappropriate techniques of production than their local counterparts in LDCs. This is true whether appropriateness is defined on the basis of physical characteristics or the profitability of techniques. Of course, most attempts to test this hypothesis have concentrated on comparing capital intensity, variously measured (including fixed assets per worker, value added per worker, and energy consumption per worker), between foreign and locally owned firms. But as argued above, we need to consider several other characteristics of technology, including elasticity of substitution, skill mix, output elasticity of inputs, scale, and sources of raw materials[24] to be able to judge appropriateness of technology. This is necessary to ensure that selection of some characteristics to maximize profits, and hence promote efficient economic growth, does not lead to a premature judgement that they are inappropriate.

The evidence is mixed when inappropriateness of technology is judged by the degree of capital intensity. Surveying twenty-seven studies on capital intensity, Waldorf (n.d.: 100) finds that 'The one thing we can conclude – with certainty – . . . is that the findings are inconclusive.' He comes to this conclusion because while some studies found foreign firms to be significantly more capital-intensive than local firms, others found no statistically significant differences between them. In some other cases, local firms were significantly more capital-intensive than foreign firms. But from studies in which observations were standardized for firm size and/or product, he concludes that MNCs were more capital-intensive than local firms.[25]

From a similar survey, White (1978: 45)[26] also concludes:

> The evidence is clearly mixed. Although the MNCs may not be the heroes of appropriate technology, they are far from the villains that many make them out to be. They have the management expertise, and they are frequently willing to use it to adapt to labour-intensive processes.

Later studies have reported similar results. They include Tyler (1978) on Brazil, Lecraw (1979) and Panchareon (1980) on Thailand, Chee (1980) on Malaysia, Schive (1980) on Taiwan, Soediyono (1980) on Indonesia, Chen (1983a and b) on Hong Kong, and Ahiakpor (1986a) on Ghana.

However, when the data are further disaggregated by ownership, local state-owned firms (wholly state or mixed state–private foreign) often are the most capital-intensive, followed by foreign, and private local firms (see, for example, Tyler 1978; Ahiakpor 1986a). These results seem to be consistent with the fact that state-owned firms acquire (financial) capital at lower interest than private-sector firms, and are under less pressure to earn or maximize profits. For some of such enterprises, it is also part of their mandate to adopt modern capital-intensive techniques of production.[27] This may also explain why Pickett *et al.* (1974) and Wells (1975) could claim to have found the hands of 'engineering-men' in the selection of techniques by some state-owned firms in Ghana and Indonesia, respectively.

The size distribution of firms also tends to follow that of capital intensity. Indeed, significant positive correlations have been found between scale (variously measured, including gross value added, value of sales, and number of employees) and capital intensity, suggesting non-homotheticity of the underlying technology employed by both local and foreign firms, especially in manufacturing enterprises (see, for example, Lipsey *et al.* 1978; Tyler 1978; Lim 1979; Ahiakpor 1986a).

As in the case of capital intensity, tests of differences in the size of foreign and local firms have yielded mostly mixed or statistically insignificant results, e.g. Mason (1973) for Mexico and the Philippines, Riedel (1975) for Taiwan, Ahiakpor (1981, 1986b) for Ghana, and Chen (1983a and b) for Hong Kong. But when the data are disaggregated into state (public) and private ownership, as in Tyler (1978) and Ahiakpor (1986b), state-owned firms (sole or mixed state–private foreign) often are the largest, followed by private foreign firms. Private local firms typically are the smallest.

But the data do not indicate that capital intensity due to large scale is always greater for foreign firms than for their local counterparts. A test of that hypothesis yielded mostly statistically insignificant results (Ahiakpor 1981: 165–6), and in two cases where significant differences were found at the 5 per cent level, foreign firms became less capital-intensive as scale increased.[28]

The number of studies reporting tests of differences in the elasticities of capital–labour substitution between foreign and local firms is rather small. This may be partly due to the relatively poor quality of or difficulty of obtaining firm-level data in LDCs. But the paucity of such studies also may be due to considerable skepticism among some analysts about the suitability of applying neoclassical models to LDC data, leading to fewer studies being published.[29] For example, a referee's argument for recommending rejection of an article reporting tests of differences in capital intensity and elasticities of substitution for foreign and local firms in an LDC (submitted to a journal devoted to development studies in 1982), was that 'the author bases himself to a considerable extent on the results of regression estimates for CES functions'. And the referee had 'serious doubts on the meaning and usefulness of [the] results'. The referee supported his/her reservation with earlier 'criticism of the use of this kind of econometric [estimation] in connection with research which deals with [the] question of factor-intensities, factor-substitution, etc.' by Morawetz (1974) and Gaude (1981). To the referee's mind, the criticisms and 'empirical shortcomings' of the CES model 'lead to the conclusion, *outrightly*, that the use of such methods is so questionable that they should be rejected as analytical tools for the kind of questions' addressed in the article (my emphasis).

But published estimates of differences in the elasticities substitution between capital and labour indicate mostly mixed or statistically insignificant results. For example, Chen (1983b: 109) finds close, but slightly higher elasticities for local firms in three industries (textiles, plastics, and electronics) in Hong Kong. He did not test directly for statistical significance of the differences. However, in one industry (garments) where the coefficient appears significantly different, the elasticity for foreign firms is higher. Chen (1983b: 110), therefore, concludes that

> foreign firms in Hong Kong manufacturing use technologies very similar to those of local firms in terms of factor proportions. If the choice of technology tends to differ, it is likely that foreign firms have chosen more appropriate technologies than local firms.

Panchareon (1980), whose results for Thailand are reproduced in Chen (1983: 158), finds higher elasticities of substitution for local firms in two industries (textiles and electronics), but the reverse in one other (food). He also did not test directly for the statistical significance of the differences.

In his study of Brazilian manufacturing industries, Tyler (1978) finds the elasticity of substitution to be almost three times as large for foreign firms as for local firms. (He did not disaggregate the data by product groups.) Most of the differences in elasticity estimated by Ahiakpor (1981) for twelve Ghanaian manufacturing industries were statistically insignificant at the 5 per cent level, but of four cases where significant differences could be found, foreign firms show smaller elasticities in three (Ahiakpor 1981: 110–15).[30] However, Lipsey *et al.* (1978: 68) report higher elasticities of substitution for MNCs (US affiliates) than local firms in eight out of ten industries in a number of LDCs, and conclude that 'multinational firms have more flexibility in the choice of techniques of production than their domestic counterparts'.

Thus, in spite of the mixed results and differences in estimation techniques, including levels of aggregation, there may be good grounds for accepting Tyler's (1978: 374) conclusion that there is 'a relative advantage for foreign firms in growing and coping with a changing economic environment [in LDCs]', which the higher elasticities found by some analysts would suggest. Tyler's conclusion also appears to be consistent with the fact that foreign firms are usually more familiar with a wider variety of production techniques than local firms in LDCs. But the fact that some studies have found higher elasticities of substitution for local firms also should caution against strong generalizations from the reported evidence.

Studies reporting estimated differences in skill mix between foreign and local firms are difficult to summarize because of the different measures of skill mix used. Some have compared skilled personnel among production workers or 'operatives', while others have included professionals and managerial employees among the skilled group. Thus, depending on the measurement used, foreign firms may appear to employ a greater or lesser skill mix than local firms. For example, Mason's study based on Mexico and the Philippines data (cited in Waldorf, n.d.: 113–15) indicates considerable variation in skill mix among sectors, but often a substantially higher proportion of 'skilled' workers employed by local firms than MNCs. Similar variations exist in the data on 'technical', 'professional', and 'executive' classes of employees, although the differences are not as great.

Waldorf (n.d.: 113) interprets Mason's findings as being consistent with the hypothesis that MNCs 'tend to substitute physical capital for middle-management skills'. He also finds the results to be consistent with those of Forsyth and Solomon, who conclude: 'Clearly, PIF's [Private Indigenous Firms] show a marked tendency to employ an unusually high proportion of technical supervisory and managerial staff' in Ghana (Waldorf n.d.: 116). Vaitsos's evidence on Peru reported in Waldorf (n.d.: 118) also suggests no clear pattern of the difference in skill mix between foreign and local firms, except an apparently greater preference by foreign firms for skilled personnel with a university education.

But evidence from Singapore (cited in Waldorf n.d.: 120) shows a higher proportion of 'managers and supervisors' as well as 'clerks and sales' personnel being hired by wholly-owned Singaporean firms than firms with foreign participation. On the other hand, firms with foreign participation employed a higher proportion of technical staff and skilled and semi-skilled workmen. Concentrating solely on the share of professional workers in the labour force, Ahiakpor (1989b) finds that, on average, mixed state–foreign firms and others with foreign participation were the most skill-intensive, followed by state and private local firms in Ghana. But the data indicate considerable variation among the eleven industries studied. In general, therefore, the evidence warrants considerable caution in generalizing about differences in skill mix between foreign and local firms in LDCs.

Evidence on the sources of raw materials suggests that foreign firms are more dependent on imported raw materials than are local firms in manufacturing industries. For example, Riedel (1975) and Biersteker (1978) find 'import dependence' to be a statistically significant discriminating factor between foreign and local firms in Taiwan and Nigeria, respectively, and foreign firms to have imported a higher proportion of raw materials than local firms.[31] Hughes and Seng (1969) also find that foreign firms in Singapore, on average, imported more than 90 per cent of their raw materials, as against about 60 per cent by local firms. Cohen (1973) and Jo (1976) report similar evidence for South Korea, and Vaitsos (1976) for Peru. In a minority of cases, local firms import more raw materials than foreign firms, as observed in Ghana and Peru.[32] However, Reuber's (1973: 240) observation that 'a higher degree of foreign ownership may be associated with lower purchases from indigenous firms', seems to be a valid generalization from the evidence.

The above survey of the evidence does not clearly indicate that foreign firms employ more inappropriate characteristics of technology in LDCs than other ownership groups on the basis of factor proportions. They are not always the most capital- and skill-intensive, the largest in scale, the least responsive to factor price changes, or consistently the most dependent on imported raw materials. Rather the mixed characteristics found among the ownership groups indicate their ability and willingness to adopt different techniques when profitability demands them, particularly the privately owned firms.

The general responsiveness of firms to profitable opportunities appears to be reflected in the lack of significant differences in the rate of after-tax profits earned by foreign and private local firms in LDCs. However, private local firms typically earn higher rates of profit before taxes than private foreign firms, as reported in studies by Rosenthal (1973b) on Guatemala, Gershenberg (1976) on Uganda, Lall (1976) on India and Colombia, Tyler (1978), Newfarmer and Marsh (1981), and Mooney (1982) on Brazil, and Ahiakpor (1986b) on Ghana. This occurs because foreign firms are often enticed by host governments with tax holidays. Therefore, they could afford to earn lower rates of profit before taxes and yet achieve the same after-tax rate of profit as their local counterparts. Whatever edge in efficiency foreign firms may have over private local firms is thus turned into a larger scale of production.

The above explanation of the higher rates of profit for private local firms in LDCs has been missing in discussions of the findings by most researchers. Instead, anticipating foreign firms to be more efficient, hence more profitable, they have sought to explain away their findings with the alleged profits repatriation through transfer pricing by foreign firms (e.g. Lall 1980: 43–4; Natke 1985). (Recall the discussion of the transfer-pricing argument in Chapter 3.) Some other researchers simply doubt their results. For example, after reporting higher rates of profit for private local firms than foreign firms in Brazil, Tyler (1978: 361) adds:' Drawing any firm conclusions from these profit figures, or even using them for analytical purposes, is, however, impossible owing to the likelihood of a systematic bias understating the profits of foreign firms.'

But evidence does not support the transfer-pricing argument as a good explanation for the observed lower rates of profit for foreign firms. For

For example, after examining the data for Brazil, Natke (1985: 218) concludes that MNCs 'underprice and overprice imports, there are problems in the sampling process, or there is no systematic overpricing'. In other words, the hypothesis is not confirmed. Applying a sign test to the ratio of imported materials in value added and the rates of profit for foreign and local firms in Ghana, Ahiakpor (1986b: 331–2) finds no statistical basis for accepting the view that transfer pricing of imported materials is the reason for the lower estimated rates of profit for foreign firms. Similarly, Biersteker (1978: 88) finds 'no systematic use of transfer pricing in the form of overpricing of imported materials' among MNCs in Nigeria.

Thus, defining the appropriateness of the characteristics of technology on the basis of their profitability, it appears that the choices made by privately owned foreign and local firms have been the appropriate ones. In spite of the differences in factor mix, the choices also can be judged as appropriate for efficient economic growth. If capital can be borrowed at low rates of interest or equipment is subsidized, as is often the case in LDCs, it is more profitable to use capital-intensive techniques than labour-intensive ones. Where there are economies of scale, as some have found in LDC manufacturing industries (e.g. Boon 1975; Stewart 1977; Tyler 1978), it is also more profitable to adopt large-scale production. Thus, it must be the limited access to capital and limited management capabilities of private local firms, as well as the higher profit taxes they pay, which limit their size as compared with foreign firms.

Foreign firms may also have a greater knowledge of alternative (foreign) sources of raw materials than local firms.[33] If this is the case, then it is more efficient for the economy that they choose the cheapest sources, whether foreign or local. The so-called 'backward-linkage' effects argued by advocates of reliance on domestic raw materials may well be negative if restriction of firms to only local materials leads to higher production costs, poorer quality products, and lower profits.[34] Similarly, it may be more efficient for the economy to use a high skill-mix if it is more profitable and creates a greater demand for other local factors. In the long term, that would be a better alternative to settling for lower wealth (value added) creation through the employment of only low-skilled local labour.

The above explanations of the choices of techniques conflict with some of those found in the literature, but I think they are more consistent explanations than those founded on the irrational behaviour of firms, including engineering-man mentality, self-affliction with high wages, ethnic pride, or other forms of non-profit maximizing behaviour (see, for example, Morawetz 1974; Pickett *et al.* 1974; Wells 1975; Winston 1979). The profit-maximizing explanations also help in designing more consistent policies for efficient economic growth and development.

However, the profit-maximizing explanations do not apply equally to the techniques chosen by state-owned firms, since these do not typically operate under the profit/loss incentive system; they are often the largest and least profitable firms in LDCs (see, for example, Tyler 1978 (Brazil); Perkins 1983 (Tanzania); Ahiakpor 1986b (Ghana)). Their losses, which they frequently make, are borne by tax-payers, and their production activities reflect mainly the political preferences of those in government, not those of participants in the marketplace. By diverting capital to less profitable activities, these firms retard economic growth, and ultimately development. Thus, although their choices of technological characteristics may be in response to their peculiar circumstances, those choices frequently are inappropriate for efficient economic development.

Summary

This long chapter deserves a summary. Appropriateness of technology should be decided on a combination of production characteristics and their effect on the profitability of firms. On that basis, there is little evidence to support the charge of inappropriate choices, either for foreign or private local firms. Instead foreign firms, like their local counterparts, are responsive to economic incentives and choose characteristics of technology consistent with profit maximization. Since profits are the most important foundation of economic growth, their choices must thus be judged appropriate. A change of incentives for state-owned firms from social/political considerations to profitability would also ensure that their choices of techniques are appropriate for efficient economic growth and development.

The role of incentives in determining the selection of techniques in LDCs has been widely recognized in the literature, prompting the call for governments in these countries to get prices 'right'. If the functioning of the economy is to reflect the wishes of market participants (or asset owners) then the required policy is that of non-government intervention in setting prices. Even in the face of government-distorted market prices, I argue that the techniques selected in response to them are still appropriate on the grounds of profitability. Resort to shadow prices as the basis for selecting 'appropriate' techniques tends to produce lower actual profits or losses and retard economic growth and, ultimately, development.

There is also little merit to the charge of inappropriate choice of products manufactured by MNCs. This charge derives from paternalism or the collectivist ideology of the advocates of an 'appropriate' products policy for LDCs. Furthermore, there is no valid theoretical argument to suggest that subjecting people in LDCs to inferior quality products would promote a faster economic growth or development. But there are good reasons for arguing that such a policy would be detrimental to economic growth and the feeling of well-being among the population of these countries. Respect for the preferences of individuals in LDCs also warrants no such claims.

Chapter five

Multinational corporations, LDC exports and development

One of the anticipated benefits from foreign direct investment by MNCs is their being more able to sell in the more developed countries (MDCs) than LDC firms. This advantage is expected to come from the special tariff privileges MNCs tend to enjoy from their home governments. For example, imports of US firms from related companies (affiliates) attract lower tariffs under US law (see Helleiner 1979). Also in 1982, about 43 per cent of the value of US imports under such special treatment (tariff item 807) came from LDCs (Helleiner 1988). Furthermore, partly under this inducement, over 32 per cent of all imports into the US in 1974 came from affiliates of US corporations (Hood and Young 1979: 171). Cohen (1973: 190) also cites evidence of a more than doubling of 'exports from LDC's by foreign affiliates of United States manufacturing firms' between 1965 and 1968, about 33 per cent average annual growth. Thus, it has been suggested that LDCs may look upon MNCs as their representatives in the 'court' of trade regulation in MDCs. The relative export advantage of MNCs is also expected from their greater familiarity with marketing techniques in MDCs as compared with their local counterparts in LDCs.

The tariff-advantage view of MNCs' exporting capabilities seems reasonable, given the inclination of governments sometimes to take into account arguments of local firms regarding the negative consequences of import tariffs on their production costs. Firms may blame high import tariffs for rising production costs and impairment of their ability to create more employment at home. But job-losses also could be used as an argument in favour of restrictive tariffs on imports if local firms are not dependent on foreign manufactures as inputs in their own production. For example, it is quite common for MDC governments to impose high import duties on manufactured textiles from LDCs in response to requests for protection by domestic textile industries.

On the other hand, some analysts have expressed serious reservations on the expectation of growth-promoting effects of MNC exports. They argue that MNCs may rather restrict the export potential of an economy if such restrictions fit within the global-marketing activities of the parent company. According to this argument, one method of minimizing competition for the market of goods and services produced by MNCs is for them to buy up their competitors as affiliates. It is exports from LDCs that are restrained in such cases. (This argument is besides the claim that foreign firms use the exporting process to transfer excessive profits from LDCs.)

Under some conditions, both the positive and negative views of MNCs' exporting activities may be valid. The difficulty is in determining which of the conditions is more likely to prevail. Furthermore, if the positive view is more valid, there are still questions of appropriate policy by host governments towards MNCs. Should MNCs receive special privileges in order to promote LDC exports? Should such incentives be extended to local firms? On a more general level, must LDC governments actively promote exports as an instrument of development policy? The answer to all three questions seems to be 'no' if LDCs seek to promote efficient economic development. I explain the answer in this chapter after first examining the relationship between the growth of exports and economic growth.

Exports and economic growth

One of the enduring propositions in economics is the so-called 'vent-for-surplus' theory of international trade (e.g. Myint 1958; Ingham 1979). According to this revived version of Adam Smith's argument in favour of free trade, the main benefit from international trade lies in the greater market it affords the surplus produce of a country. Foreign trade thus enables producers to earn a higher income than would otherwise be possible. In Smith's own words, 'Without such exportation, a part of the productive labour of the country must cease, and the value of its annual produce diminish' (Smith 1976: 1: 394).

But Smith did not imply that producers would be so unwise as to produce articles for which they did not first anticipate the existence of demand. Such an interpretation would be inconsistent with his self-interest axiom of commercial activity (e.g. Smith 1976: 1: 18). Smith was concerned with the negative consequences of mercantilist trade regulation by government. Therefore, the correct interpretation of his 'vent-for-surplus' argument ought to be a call for free enterprise. It is the greater freedom from trade restrictions that enables producers and sellers (as a whole) to earn higher incomes.

However, the expectation of greater income from foreign trade has led some governments to actively promote exports as a development policy. The policy has often taken the form of export subsidies, especially to manufacturing enterprises (lower tariff on inputs for processing for re-export and lower taxes on profits from exports), undervaluation of exchange rates to make exports more attractive in foreign markets, as well as the creation of export processing zones (EPZs) in which different tax and other commercial laws apply than in the rest of the economy.[1] Notable among countries that have adopted these incentive schemes are Barbados, India, Malaysia, Mauritius, Singapore, and Sri Lanka. For example, incentives to promote exports in Malaysia include 'an export allowance, an accelerated depreciation allowance and double deduction of overseas promotional expenses' extending between 10 and 12 years, and 'import duty exemption for machinery and industrial raw materials' (Ariff and Lim 1987: 108). Under the same impetus, profits from exports attract a 4 per cent tax instead of the usual 40 per cent in Singapore (Fong 1987: 86).

Several attempts have been made to evaluate indirectly the wisdom of such incentives for promoting exports in LDCs. One is a test of the relationship between a country's economic growth and export growth (e.g. Emery 1967; Maizels 1968: 41–9; Kravis 1970). The intent is to detect the existence of a 'pull-effect' on the economy from export growth. The results indeed have indicated a positive relationship between exports and economic growth, but, as Michaely (1977) has argued, no other results could have been obtained from such a test since exports are part of national income. He thus suggests a more meaningful test, which is to correlate the growth of real per capita income with the growth of exports as a share of national output (also see Ram 1987).[2] This test, in general, has also yielded a positive association between export growth and national income growth.

The results also reveal a disturbing pattern: the positive influence of exports on income growth has been observed mainly among middle-income LDCs; among low-income LDCs, the results often show a negative relationship between export growth and income growth.[3] Yet for some of these countries, exports constitute more than 20 per cent of national income, e.g. Ghana, Sri Lanka, Uganda, and Zaire.[4] Thus Michaely (1977: 52) concludes that although a positive association of 'growth with export expansion [in general] has . . . been established', such a relationship holds 'only once the countries achieve some minimum level of development'. Tyler (1981: 124) also makes the same point, but, as will be argued below, this unsatisfactory conclusion is the product of an inappropriate test design.

The test of whether countries with larger shares of exports in national income grow faster than those with smaller shares has produced negative results (Michaely 1977). Indeed, while some countries in his sample experienced more than 3 per cent real annual per capita income growth with a small export share (less than 10 per cent) in national income (e.g. Brazil, South Korea, and Turkey), others with more than 25 per cent export share also recorded similar positive growth in real income (e.g. Cyprus, Iraq, Malta, and Panama). Similar evidence can also be found in Maizels (1968) and Goncalves and Richtering (1987). Finally, tests of causality between exports and national income growth have also failed to confirm the notion that export growth leads to or 'causes' economic growth (e.g. Ram 1987).

But the above tests have not correctly examined the hypothesis that export growth exerts a positive influence on economic growth because the test designs are inappropriate for discovering the relationship being sought. Had the purposiveness of individual producers been sufficiently taken into account in constructing the tests, it might have been recognized that testing with such aggregate data would not produce meaningful results.

Few producers would pass up the opportunity to earn higher incomes by selling more goods both at home and abroad. A test of that hypothesis should be one that estimates the responsiveness of producers to incentives for increased sales both at home and abroad. Thus, whether foreign trade promotes overall economic growth or not must depend mainly on the overall system of incentives under which such trade occurs. And where greater access to foreign markets is not coupled with the removal of restrictions on efficient domestic production and sale, more exports may not lead to greater total income growth.

The above argument may be explained as follows: the amount of capital (savings) accumulated in a country is fixed at a point in time. Therefore, the use of capital to produce items for domestic consumption must deny its availability for export-goods production, and vice versa. Any special incentives granted to export-goods producers amounts to allocating more of the economy's fixed capital stock to that sector at the expense of others. If incentives are offered to a sector because its production would otherwise be less profitable, such incentives must consign the economy to a slower growth path than would have occurred otherwise. Therefore, the appropriate test of the 'exports-growth nexus', as it is sometimes called, ought to be between incentive systems (both for exports and domestic production) and overall economic growth. Such a test also appears more relevant to policymaking than those so far conducted, especially the ones based on aggregate production function models (e.g. Helleiner 1988; Goncalves and Richtering 1987; Ram 1985, 1987).

The relationship between incentive systems and economic growth is also the basis of Johnson's (1967) immiserization hypothesis of sectoral protection by government, as further elaborated on by Brecher and Diaz-Alejandro (1977).[5] The latter, however, have couched their argument in terms that make foreign firms look like the villains in immiserizing LDCs through their alleged greater efficiency or profit-making than local firms (also see Helleiner 1988). But a correct appreciation of Smith's argument would lead to testing the hypothesis that a more liberal economic regime, including free access to foreign markets (both for exports and imports) promotes greater economic growth. As Smith pointed out, under free enterprise

> All systems either of preference or of restraint . . . being thus completely taken away, the obvious and simple system of natural liberty establishes itself of its own accord. Every man . . . is left perfectly free to pursue his own interest his own way, and to bring both his industry and capital into competition with those of any other man, or order of men . . . and . . . directing [them] towards the employment most suitable to the interest of the society.
>
> (Smith 1976: 2: 208)

Of course, recognition of the export-growth hypothesis as one of a relation between overall incentives and economic growth has been noted by others. For example, one of three alternative explanations Krueger (1980: 291) gives for the better economic performance of export-oriented LDCs is that 'the commitment to an export-oriented development strategy implies a fairly liberal and efficient trade regime, and thus prevents paperwork, delays, bureaucratic regulation, and other costs that can arise under import-substitution'. This is a small step from designating one strategy as enterprise-restricting (import-substitution) and the other as enterprise-freeing (export-oriented). Cable and Persaud (1987: 13) are more clear in their statement of the point, arguing: 'purely export-oriented investment is, in itself, likely to be very elusive, and *what is really at issue is the degree of market liberalisation as a whole*' (my emphasis).

The search for statistical confirmation of the positive influence of exports on economic growth, as it has so far been done, may have arisen from a misinterpretation of Smith's argument in favour of the freedom of enterprise, including trade in foreign markets or with foreigners. Granted that individuals engaged in production would take advantage of opportunities to sell as much and at the highest price as buyers would accept, a greater access to foreign markets can only lead to more output and higher incomes. If greater output reduced prices and incomes, the self-interest of producers would again cause at least some to leave the lower-profits industry and employ their capitals elsewhere. This proposition cannot meaningfully be tested with the kind of aggregate data that have been used, especially when the policy instruments affecting individual behaviour are excluded from the test design.

The contribution of MNCs to LDC export growth

It is an empirical question whether MNCs contribute significantly to the growth of exports in LDCs, but statistical evidence to verify this fact is not easy to find since most published country data tend to lump MNCs with other foreign-owned firms. Thus, unless explicitly stated, the discussion below refers to foreign firms in general.

If the data could be found, we can anticipate that the significance of foreign firms in promoting LDC exports would depend on the country's resource endowment, predominant production technology, level of development, and government policy. Foreign firms would feature prominently in the production and export of goods based on such natural resources as oil and gas, and minerals such as gold, copper, diamond, and bauxite, if host country governments do not prohibit their entry or restrict their activities in such industries. On the other hand, cultivation and export of such tropical crops as bananas, cocoa, coffee, pineapples, rubber, and tea may be undertaken by foreign firms, including MNCs, depending on whether they are grown on plantations. However, foreign firms may still engage in the export of these crops as buyers from local small-scale growers, although not on the same scale as from direct cultivation.

The focus on MNCs and their role in export promotion in LDCs has been in the area of manufactures, or what are known as 'non-traditional exports'. But their contribution to such exports, and to national income growth, depends very much on the level of the country's development, that is, more in middle-income and less in low-income LDCs. For middle-income LDCs the share of manufactures in national income on average ranged from 17 per cent (lower-middle-income) to 35 per cent (upper-middle-income) in 1985 (World Bank 1987: 206–27). For low-income LDCs, excluding China and India, the average share of manufactures in national income was just about 12 per cent. (Figures for China and India are 37 and 17 per cent, respectively.) Agriculture (along with services) is the dominant contributor to the national income in most low-income countries, averaging 36 per cent in 1985, compared with 22 per cent for lower-middle-income countries, and 10 per cent in upper-middle-income LDCs.

The share of manufactures in exports is even smaller for most LDCs, although a few countries have been quite successful in exporting manufactures. Significant among the low-income LDCs with exceptional manufactured exports performance in 1985, for example, are India (49 per cent), China (54 per cent), Pakistan (63 per cent), and Bangladesh (65 per cent) (see World Bank 1987). The performance of the following countries also stand out among middle-income LDCs: the Philippines (51 per cent), Turkey (54 per cent), Singapore (58 per cent), Korea (91 per cent), and Hong Kong (92 per cent). Thus, for low-income LDCs, excluding China and India, manufactures on average amount to about 24 per cent of exports, of which 13 per cent are textiles (1985). (Values for China and India together are 52 per cent of manufactures, of which

23 per cent were textiles.) For the lower-middle-income LDCs, manufactures make up 20 per cent of exports, of which just 7 per cent are textiles, while upper-middle-income LDCs have average percentages of 48 per cent and 9 per cent, respectively.

The high variation in the percentages of manufactures in total exports among LDCs is also partly an indication of the varying degrees of export incentives offered in some of these countries. The relative ability of foreign firms to take advantage of such incentives or the degree to which the incentives are targeted more at foreign firms would explain their export performance in manufactures as compared with local firms. For example, Newfarmer (1983: 180) notes evidence of greater 'export propensity' among MNCs than local firms in the engineering industries of Mexico. He attributes this to the government's 'carrot-and-stick measures to create' export incentives for foreign firms. Similarly greater export performance by MNCs in the automobiles industry of Mexico is reported by Bennett and Sharpe (1979a and b).

Other studies reporting better export performance of foreign firms or MNCs include Cohen (1973, 1975) and Jo (1976) for Korea, de la Torre (1974) for Colombia, Mexico, and Nicaragua, Rosenthal (1973b) for Guatemala, Willmore (1976) for Costa Rica, Fong (1987) for Singapore, Wanigatunga (1987) for Sri Lanka, and Worrell *et al.* (1987) for Barbados. But some studies have found little or no difference between the share of manufactured exports by foreign and locally owned firms. These include Cohen (1975) for Taiwan, and Newfarmer and Marsh (1981) for Brazil. Yet others have reported greater exports by local firms than foreign ones. They include Vaitsos (1978) for Argentina, Brazil, Colombia, Mexico, Peru, and Venezuela, Cohen (1975) for Singapore, Fajnzylber and Martinez-Tarrago (1976) for Mexico, Lall and Streeten (1977) for Colombia, India, Iran, Jamaica, Kenya, and Malaysia, and Westphal *et al.* (1979) for Korea.

What we can conclude from the above survey of the evidence is that the record of foreign firms' performance in exporting manufactures compared with that of local firms in LDCs is mixed. In the same country, the evidence may also change over time or between industries, as indicated by the apparently conflicting conclusions regarding Mexico (Bennett and Sharpe, 1979a and b; Vaitsos, 1978; Newfarmer, 1983) and for Singapore (Cohen, 1975; Fong, 1987). But, as argued below, there is no particular reason why foreign firms must export more (or fewer) manufactures than their local counterparts. Whatever evidence is observed can be explained by the theory of foreign direct investment.

Some of the conflicting conclusions may have arisen from differences in test design or the peculiar interpretations of the evidence by the researchers. They must thus be treated with caution. For example, if the measure of export performance is 'percentage of sales exported' (e.g. Lall and Streeten, 1977) without controlling for scale, the conclusion may be biased against foreign firms. As discussed in Chapter 4, foreign firms are typically larger than local firms in LDCs, except sometimes state-owned enterprises. Thus, although some private local firms may export a larger share of their output, this may amount to a smaller volume of exports than those of foreign firms. Therefore, 'export propensity' has to be distinguished from the volume of sales when assessing the relative contributions of foreign and local firms to exports.

The conclusion by Lall and Streeten (1977: 135) that *'foreign control does not generally seem to promote exports and may even inhibit it'*, appears to be one of those unwarranted by the evidence, yet claimed by some researchers (emphasis in original). They base their claim on evidence indicating that of eighty-eight MNCs operating in Colombia, India, Iran, Jamaica, Kenya, and Malaysia, twenty-three (or 26 per cent) exported none of their output. But as many as thirty-three (or 47 per cent) of seventy-one non-MNCs in the data exported nothing either. Grouping the same data into foreign and local firms, we find that forty-six (35 per cent) of 133 foreign firms exported nothing as compared with ten (39 per cent) of twenty-six locally controlled firms. Clearly the proportion of firms exporting nothing is greater among locally controlled firms.

Of firms whose exports amounted up to 9 per cent of their sales, fifty-three (60 per cent) are MNCs while twenty-four (34 per cent) are non-MNCs. Figures for the foreign and locally controlled groups are sixty-five (50 per cent) and twelve firms (46 per cent) respectively. Finally, eleven MNCs (12 per cent) exported more than 10 per cent of their sales as compared with fifteen non-MNCs (21 per cent), while twenty-two foreign-controlled firms (17 per cent) compared with four locally-controlled firms (15 per cent) exported more than 10 per cent of their sales. Thus, even without adjusting the data for differences in the volume of exports, the evidence hardly warrants Lall and Streeten's conclusion that the presence of foreign-controlled firms may inhibit exports from LDCs.[6] Such a conclusion also suggests that the presence of foreign firms prevents even domestic firms from exporting some of their output. It is hard to believe that the authors could have meant this.

Reconciling evidence with the theory of MNCs

Whether foreign firms export more or less of their output than local firms really depends on their reasons for locating production plants abroad (e.g. Agarwal 1980). This assertion holds even in the face of ample evidence that MNCs have a greater relative ability to sell in developed country markets than LDC firms.

To demonstrate the validity of the above claim, recall the prime motive of the firm, namely, to make the most profits possible. As I argued in Chapter 2, the firm's path to profit-making may be inhibited by government policies, notably taxes on transactions. For example, in the absence of import duties, a foreign firm may find it more profitable to export goods through wholesalers at home or sell abroad through its own retailing outlets. However, if import duties are imposed, they raise the cost of such transactions to the foreign firm. Thus by raising the selling prices, import duties reduce the volume of goods foreign firms can sell abroad while enabling local firms to sell more (and perhaps at cheaper prices). If production abroad is intended to jump over this tariff wall, foreign firms would have no particular advantage to export what they produce in the tariff-protected country. For example, most foreign firms interviewed in Malaysia cited production for sale in the Malaysian market rather than for export as the most important motive for their investment there (Ariff and Lim 1987: 106). Low labour costs, which one might have expected to be an incentive for manufacturing for export in Malaysia, ranked only third in importance for US and European firms.

Indeed, the fact that the foreign firm did not locate its production in a country until the imposition of import tariffs indicates the relative cost disadvantage it originally must have faced. There are transaction costs such as understanding a foreign legal system, dealing with foreign government bureaucracy, understanding foreign language and culture in order to handle employee problems efficiently, finding skilled personnel to handle modern (foreign-firm) technology, or the costs of adapting modern technology to the conditions of a foreign country. As suggested in Chapter 3, these transactions costs can outweigh whatever technological advantages such firms may have over their local counterparts. Thus, in the absence of any other inducement to export manufactures apart from tax incentives, foreign firms may not export more than local firms.

We also noted in Chapter 3 that access to cheap raw materials or labour, or securing a stable flow of materials could be the reason for foreign firms to locate in LDCs. These indeed were the second most important set of reasons given by Japanese firms for locating in Malaysia.[7] In such a case, manufacturing for export may be an important reason for foreign direct investment (FDI).

A third kind of 'inducement' for foreign firms to produce abroad for export is increased transactions costs imposed by tariffs on the export of unprocessed materials (e.g. log timber or unprocessed cocoa beans). This situation frequently arises where Third World governments pursue an export-promotion policy based on the notion that processed or manufactured exports earn higher net revenues in foreign exchange than unprocessed exports. Frequently the calculation of foreign exchange earnings from exports in such cases is based not on earnings per domestic factor costs, but on gross receipts. Thus after deducting the higher domestic production costs, including the cost of imported machinery, sometimes imported skilled personnel, and royalties for use of imported technology, net foreign exchange earnings from manufactures may be less than those from the export of raw materials.

But without financial inducements for foreign firms, the higher transactions costs imposed by the export tariff may succeed only in limiting the volume of domestic raw materials utilized by the firms. It may also cause a fall in net revenue from manufactured exports of the product involved. However, given their prior involvement in the sale of manufactures based on such products abroad, foreign firms may still have an exporting advantage over their local counterparts.

If subsidies and other inducements are given to firms to encourage exports of manufactures from a tariff-protected country, the country as a whole may be losing income. The concessions amount to trading domestic resources at a loss or for a lower return with foreigners, by the extent of the subsidies. Although more domestic resources may thereby be employed in the affected industries, they would be employed at the expense of other industries in which they could have generated higher revenues over cost (productivity). Furthermore, under the usual cost conditions, payment to the firm's hired domestic factors (or resources) could be less than the value of inducement received. Thus such exports may well be profitable to firms receiving the inducements, but they can hardly be to the advantage of the community as a whole. It may be suggested that modern technology or manufacturing skills could be acquired through subsidizing production for export – an infant-industry type of argument. But finding cheaper means or more direct ways of paying for the desired technology or skills may be a more economically efficient approach.

Finally, it may be argued that granting incentives to promote exports would generate more foreign exchange or relax the country's 'foreign-exchange constraint' on development. However, as I pointed out in Chapter 3, the foreign-exchange constraint argument (including the notion of a foreign-exchange gap) stems from either a misconception of the development process or failure to confront directly bad or inconsistent economic policies in several LDCs, particularly fixed and overvalued exchange rates.

The only true source of acquiring foreign exchange in any country is from production and sale of goods and services to foreigners. Even the inflow of foreign investment (direct or portfolio) constitutes sale of assets by residents of the recipient country to foreigners. Considering that the ultimate purpose of production is consumption, the sale of domestically produced goods and services to foreigners must indicate the extent to which domestic residents want to acquire other things produced more cheaply by foreigners.[8] And unless the price of foreign exchange is fixed by the government, the exchange of goods and services, including IOUs, would be self-equilibrating. At the existing market exchange rate, the amount of goods and services desired by foreigners would just equal the amount willingly supplied by domestic residents.

Thus, short of borrowing from foreigners, the only sure way of obtaining more foreign exchange is for nationals to sell more domestic goods and services. If instead of nationals, sales are made abroad by resident foreign producers, only the portion due to domestic factors really constitutes an addition to the country's stock of foreign exchange. Although in an accounting sense export proceeds accrue to the country of export, the ownership or property rights attached to them are quite different. Unless foreigners have been expropriated of incomes they have earned, not all of the proceeds belong to the recipient country. This is why it is a misperception of reality to argue that income repatriation by foreign firms constitutes a drain on the host country's stock of foreign exchange.

Subsidizing foreign firms so they can export more amounts to granting them more right to the foreign exchange thus earned, at the expense of the country's nationals. But this could hardly have been the intention of the incentive programme in the first place. Granting subsidies to domestic producers is not a good alternative either. The policy would assign to recipients of the subsidies a greater command over foreign exchange without ensuring that more net foreign exchange would be earned.

It is because of the above reasons that I answer 'no' to the questions posed at the beginning of this chapter, including the question, should MNCs receive special incentives to promote manufactured exports from LDCs? Such incentives may distort the country's economy into producing less cost-efficient products. The incentives also do not guarantee higher net foreign-exchange earnings per unit of exports. It would be a more efficient policy if, as argued by Adam Smith, all systems of preference or restraint were removed to allow firms to engage in the most profitable production, and for sale in the most rewarding markets, foreign or domestic.

Chapter six

Multinationals and efficiency in resource utilization

The economic development consequences of production by multinational corporations or foreign firms in a host country depend on the efficiency with which they employ resources at their disposal. We need not approach this issue from a worldview perspective; for host countries such a perspective is of little relevance. Rather, it is the use of resources to which citizens have ownership claims that is of significance. Such resources include savings or financial capital, raw materials, land, and labour. There are opportunity costs to their employment by MNCs in terms of the output that would have been created had they been employed by local firms.

Ascertaining whether local firms would have utilized the resources employed by foreign firms or MNCs is difficult. Indeed, in the absence of MNCs some resources may not be employed or utilized. If so, the very presence of foreign firms may be a net benefit for the economy. (Operations of foreign firms may create a net loss for an economy if the firms had been enticed with financial incentives that outweigh their payments to domestic factors.) Where both foreign and local firms operate within the same industry, differences in their utilization of resources may be used to approximate their relative contributions to the growth of the host economy.

Unlike most other aspects of the debate over the development consequences of MNC presence in the less-developed countries, most analysts argue an efficiency advantage for these firms. The argument proceeds from the premise that foreign firms employ more advanced technologies (or techniques) in production than local firms. It is from the same assumption that some argue an exploitation theory of MNC activities in LDCs. Having superior technology in terms of management, production processes, and marketing, so goes the argument, these firms outperform local firms in earning profits, which they then repatriate, to the detriment of indigenous development potential (e.g. Dos Santos 1970; Hymer 1979, especially chapters 1 and 2; Bornschier 1980). This is the so-called 'decapitalization' hypothesis of MNC activities in LDCs.

(See, for example, Jackman 1982; Ahiakpor 1986b, for some statistical rebuttal of the argument at both the macro (between countries) and micro (within country) levels.) In this chapter I review the available evidence on the differences in efficiency between foreign and local firms, and draw implications from these for economic growth in LDCs.

Measuring differences in efficiency

At least three methods may be used to measure differences in efficiency between MNCs or foreign firms and their local counterparts: (1) total factor productivity, (2) profits, and (3) partial productivity indicators such as labour or capital productivity. In principle, total factor productivity appears to be the most comprehensive and appropriate measure of efficiency. It measures the contribution of primary factors (usually capital goods and labour) to net output or value added – the value of output less material costs. However, it is a difficult index to construct with one-period data.

The difficulty arises because the service flow of capital goods does not lend itself to easy measurement. Some (e.g. Corbo and Havrylyshyn 1982) approximate the service flow by the expenditure on fuel and electricity. But the use of equipment and machinery entails much more than can be measured by energy consumption alone.[1] Furthermore, rates of capital consumption or depreciation are determined jointly by changes in the market value as well as the physical wear and tear of capital goods. Some analysts (e.g. Agarwal 1979) use the rate of dividends paid or a purely hypothetical opportunity cost of capital (Mason 1973). Still others measure total factor productivity as the ratio of the change in value added to the change in an index of primary factor inputs.

The difficulty of constructing generally acceptable one-period values of total factor productivity may explain the scarcity of studies estimating total factor productivity differences between foreign and local firms. The studies that do exist report mixed evidence, although the general thrust of their conclusions seems to be that foreign firms are more productive. For example, in his study of manufacturing industries in India, Agarwal (1979) finds significantly superior performance of foreign firms over local firms. Local firms were more productive in three industries, but the weighted average over all thirty-four industries studied show a 55 per cent higher total productivity index for foreign firms. Mason's (1973) tests of differences in total factor productivity between US and local firms in Mexico and the Philippines show US firms to be significantly more productive when the opportunity cost of capital is assumed to be 12 per cent. But the differences are no longer statistically significant when the assumed opportunity cost is 18 per cent, which he believes to be the more appropriate number.

Profits may serve the same purpose as total factor productivity in distinguishing the more efficient from less efficient firms. They summarize the efficiency of firms in their utilization of resources, including capital (financial and physical), labour, land, and materials.[2] It may be argued that firms earning higher rates of profit have employed their resources more efficiently than those earning less. In a static sense, this interpretation appears to be correct, but the production activities of firms take place within a dynamic context. Thus profit rates alone may be a misleading indicator of the relative efficiency of firms.

A firm seeking to maximize total profits increases its production when it earns a higher rate of after-tax profit at its current level of output than it could have made elsewhere. If increased production raises costs per unit of output, the rate of profit would decline. The same decline in profits occurs if costs do not increase with additional output but the firm faces a downward-sloping demand curve. That is, for the additional output to be sold, price must fall. Thus, a lower rate of profits due to a higher scale of production may be consistent with higher total profits for the firm. To infer correctly differences in efficiency from profit rates, therefore, requires the size of firms to be taken into account. Given identical rates of profit, total profits are greater for larger firms than for smaller ones.

Using total after-tax profits as the measure of relative efficiency, MNCs or foreign firms appear to be the most efficient users of resources among groups of firms in LDCs. Foreign and private local firms earn about the same rates of after-tax profit in similar industries (Ahiakpor 1986b), but foreign firms are typically more than twice as large as private local firms, whether scale is measured as value of net assets (e.g. Tyler 1978), number of employees, or gross value added (e.g. Ahiakpor 1986b).

It has been found that private local firms on average earn higher rates of gross profits than foreign firms, including MNCs (e.g. Rosenthal 1973b; Newfarmer and Marsh 1981; Ahiakpor 1986b),[3] but the difference in profit rates typically does not exceed the difference in scale of value added or sales. It appears the higher levels of profit taxes paid by private local firms, as compared with foreign firms who enjoy tax concessions or holidays, is a major reason for their smaller scale of production, but it is difficult to tell how much larger private local firms could have been if both types of firms were treated equally with respect to tax concessions. The technological advantage of MNCs, the exploitation of which leads them to locate in foreign countries, may still enable such firms to operate on a larger scale than private local firms.

The evidence also shows that state-owned firms (wholly state or joint state–foreign) operate on a much larger scale than foreign firms, including sometimes MNCs. For example, Tyler (1981) finds that in 1971 state-owned firms in Brazil were on average 27 times as large as private foreign firms. Ahiakpor (1986b) finds wholly state-owned firms in Ghana to be on average about twice as large as private foreign firms, while joint state–foreign firms were on average about five times as large in 1970.

But state-owned or joint state–foreign firms frequently make losses or typically earn much lower rates of gross profits than private foreign and local firms. Often the main preoccupation of state-owned firms is not profit maximization but employment creation, though not necessarily through choosing more labour-intensive production processes. Sometimes the objective is more to introduce modern techniques of production into the economy than to earn the highest possible profits. Therefore, judging by their lower rates of profit, or even persistent losses, wholly state- and joint state–foreign-owned firms appear to be the least efficient users of resources in LDCs.

Although a partial measure of efficiency in resource utilization, differences in the productivity of labour may be an important indicator of the relative contributions of foreign and local firms to the development of LDC economies. On this index, both theory and much of the evidence suggest that foreign firms contribute more than their local counterparts. Labour productivity is usually expected to be higher for employees of MNCs or foreign firms than local firms. The expectation is based on the argument that MNCs or foreign firms use more modern technology (by which is usually meant more modern equipment and machinery relative to labour) or they employ more modern management techniques than local firms. Mason (1973), for example, confirms this expectation with data on US MNCs operating in Mexico and the Philippines.[4] (But as explained in Chapter 4 above, foreign firms are not always the most capital-intensive in LDCs.)

An indirect test of the expectation of higher labour productivity in foreign firms is to compare average worker wages paid by foreign firms with those paid by local firms. Such a test is valid if firms attempt to equate the wages with marginal revenue product of labour in order to maximize profits or minimize costs. On this relative-wage criterion, foreign firms again appear to employ labour most productively in LDCs.

Although there are some instances in which local firms pay higher average wages than foreign firms in the same industries, the general pattern of findings is that foreign firms pay higher average wages. The findings include Hughes and Seng (1969) for Singapore, Langdon (1975) for Kenya, Jo (1976) for South Korea, Sourrouille (1976) for Argentina, Vaitsos (1976) for Peru, Forsyth and Solomon (1977) for Ghana, and Biersteker (1978) for Nigeria. Others are Sepulveda and Chumacero (1973) for Mexico, Mason (1973) for Mexico and the Philippines, Lim (1977) for Malaysia, Iyanda and Bello (1979) for Nigeria, and Possas (1979) for Brazil. However, the gap between the average wages paid by foreign and local firms narrows when the data are controlled for product type, scale, and skill mix.

On the other hand, state-owned firms in LDCs often pay higher wages than MNCs or foreign firms. This follows from attempts by governments in these countries to be leaders in setting wages in the modern sector, just as they also often try to lead in the introduction of modern production techniques. But since state-owned firms usually earn lower rates of profit than private foreign and local firms and frequently make losses, their higher wages would not necessarily reflect greater efficiency in their employment of labour.

As discussed earlier, foreign firms or MNCs earn about the same rate of after-tax profits as private local firms in LDCs. Evidence of higher wages paid by foreign firms thus suggests that, compared with their local counterparts, foreign firms are more able to derive high output per employee in return. This inference contrasts with other arguments advanced as explanations of the wage differential between foreign and local firms, including:

(a) foreign firms have a competitive advantage in product markets in LDCs and are thus able to pass higher wage costs on to consumers in the form of higher prices;

(b) foreign firms are under greater trade union pressure than local firms to pay higher wages in the same industries;

(c) foreign firms imitate the high wages paid in their home countries;

(d) foreign firms pay higher wages to maintain a good image in host LDCs (and not appear to be discriminating between local and foreign labour who otherwise would have been paid higher); and

(e) foreign firms pay higher wages to attract and retain the best workers.

Even if any of the above arguments could explain the higher wages typically paid by foreign firms at any point in time, they could not explain the persistence of the practice over time. The need to pay attractive dividends to shareholders would suggest that foreign firms obtain as much productivity as possible from workers to justify continuing to pay higher wages.

There has been little testing of the hypothesis that foreign firms pay higher wages because they obtain higher labour productivity from their employees. Dunning (1981) reports mixed results from testing the hypothesis. He uses sales per employee as an index of labour productivity and correlates this index with the ratio of wages in US affiliates and local firms. The correlation coefficient is positive and statistically significant for Mexico (1966), but he does not obtain conclusive results for six other countries, including the US, UK, Canada, and West Germany.

Testing for the correlation between growth of wages and labour productivity, Dunning (1981: 290) also finds a positive relationship 'for all countries taken together (0.65) excluding the US parent companies and non-MNEs, and (0.66) when they were included, although no country, individually, showed a significant relationship'.[5] On the whole, however, Dunning concludes from his series of tests that 'it would seem that differences in employee compensation are more significantly related to the value of net output per employee than any other cause' (p. 296). Future tests are likely to confirm the hypothesized positive correlation between labour productivity and wages, especially when value added per worker is used as the measure of productivity and less aggregated industry data than those of Dunning are employed.

Implications for economic growth

As noted above, some critics of foreign firms are concerned about the negative consequences for LDCs due to the superior efficiency of these firms in contrast with their local counterparts. They are concerned that distribution of the returns due to the relative superiority of foreign firms favours foreign inputs, such as financial and physical capital, and managerial personnel, rather than local factors. They argue that host countries might benefit more from the greater efficiency of foreign firms if the firms employed local factors, especially labour, land, and materials, and by implication earned less profits. Otherwise, they see the greater efficiency of foreign firms mainly as a means of extracting wealth from LDCs.

Where the evidence is available, differences in payments to domestic factors by foreign and local firms may be used to qualify the inference drawn from the differences in their efficiency. However, the need for such qualification is not a valid argument for insisting that firms, foreign or local, use local raw materials in their production. Unless such usage increases their profits, insistence on their purchase may lead to lower production which would also mean less hiring of local labour. To the extent that foreign firms pay taxes on their profits, government revenues from such taxes may also decline in accord with the lower profits they would make. If local resources are subsidized to encourage their purchase by foreign firms, such a policy may also cause some income loss to the economy if the resources could have been sold at higher prices on the export market.

Taking into account the distribution of the returns to the greater efficiency of foreign firms, we can still argue that the implications for economic growth in LDCs are positive. To show this, recall that revenues of the firms pay the various co-operating factors in production, namely, capital goods, land, labour, and entrepreneurship, apart from taxes. (Financial capital with which capital goods are bought and the services of land and labour are hired, receives payment out of revenues in the form of interest.) Thus, arguing over the profits of foreign firms amounts to making claims over the income of a foreign factor. It is over the payments to domestic factors that disputes may appear to be legitimate.

There is little direct evidence on the differences in rental payments for land and buildings, or prices paid for domestic raw materials by foreign firms compared with their local counterparts. Some foreign firms may be attracted to LDCs by subsidized rentals on land and buildings at government-constructed industrial estates in these countries, but in general, there is little reason to expect foreign firms to pay lower rates than their local counterparts. Indeed, local factor owners may charge foreign firms higher rentals than local firms. If so, the contributions of foreign firms to income creation for local factors would be higher.

Similarly, the generally higher wages foreign firms pay local labour must be reckoned as contributing more to domestic income creation compared with the payments of local firms. Finally, the larger size of foreign firms as compared with private local firms also suggests that they create more incomes for domestic factors per establishment than do local firms, even if the rates of payment are the same.

In summary, foreign firms, including MNCs, appear on average to be the most efficient users of resources in LDCs. Estimates of total factor productivity are higher on average for foreign firms than for local firms. Both foreign and private local firms may earn similar after-tax rates of profit, but the former are much larger than the latter. Hence the total profits of foreign firms (gross or after-tax) are typically greater than those of private local firms. State-owned firms, on the other hand, are usually the least profitable, and therefore the least efficient.

It is legitimate to examine the impact of the greater efficiency of foreign firms on host countries in terms of the incomes they create for domestic factors. In so doing, one must also recognize the legitimacy of foreign factors, including capital and entrepreneurship, to earn incomes due to them. Following this method of assessing the contributions of foreign firms to the development process of LDCs, the evidence suggests mainly positive contributions.

Trying to evaluate this conclusion further by comparing the share of foreign firms in production (value added) with the growth experience of host countries may produce misleading results, since there are other important determinants of economic growth. But the very positive growth experience of countries that have been more open to foreign direct investment, including Hong Kong, Singapore, South Korea, and Taiwan, and which also have adopted more open market-oriented policies, would suggest the benefits of foreign firms to LDCs. (See, for example, Balassa 1988; Stoever 1986; Sharma 1984 for some excellent evaluations of these experiences.) Equivalent conclusions may be drawn from the experience of the more-developed countries with foreign direct investment.

Chapter seven

Summary and conclusions

The debate over the contributions of multinational corporations to economic growth and development in LDCs arises from several sources. The arguments may be classified under (a) dispute over relevant theory, (b) dispute over interpretations of evidence, and (c) policy design. These underlying elements of the debate are not usually separated in arguments frequently encountered in the literature on multinational corporations. Rather they tend to go together. The focus of this book has been to sort out disputes over MNCs mainly on the basis of relevant economic theory and interpretations of available evidence. The third part of the debate, that is, policy design, will be taken up towards the end of this chapter, but first, a summary of the substantive arguments developed in Chapters 2–6.

The main argument presented in Chapter 2 is that the theory of a firm that explains the behaviour of a UNC is equally capable of being applied to an MNC. Thus, like a UNC, the MNC is run by an entrepreneurial group with an interest in the long-term survival of the enterprise and whose incomes depend directly on the corporation's profits performance. But for operating over geographical regions separated by different legal boundaries, the MNC would have been another UNC with branch plants.

Where currencies can be exchanged openly or through some other media established by governments, operating multi-plants across different currency zones changes very little the similarity between UNCs and MNCs. Even when currency exchanges are prohibited, MNCs would not operate abroad unless they find it profitable to do so. The task of the analyst then is to discover how their need to pay attractive dividends to shareholders of the corporation is met within different operating circumstances.

One factor which is significant in creating difficulties for analysing the behaviour of MNCs, is the definition of competition employed in modern economics, especially since the 1930s, to mean price-taking behaviour of numerous firms and consumers. If competition is defined as rivalry in the classical and early neoclassical tradition, there is no need to invoke arguments of imperfections in the marketplace, both domestic and international, to explain the operations of MNCs.[1]

The market is the reflection of choices made by individuals who are not perfect. Individuals often lack full information about relevant characteristics of goods and services they buy as well as about all existing alternatives. They also change their minds over time. Thus, a market cannot be any more perfect than its constituent individuals. Recognizing the limited usefulness of the perfect competition assumption in economics, we can substitute for it the rivalrous behaviour concept when discussing the behaviour of firms.[2] That substitution also helps to minimize or eliminate much of the dispute over whether activities of MNCs promote or lessen competition and whether they enhance or reduce welfare in host countries.

The definition of economic development is another source of debate. Unlike economic growth, which is measured as changes in some economic magnitudes, the definition of economic development takes various forms often depending on the purpose for which the concept is being used. Thus, it may be defined to include a persistent rise in real income per capita as well as the quality of life. Others may include increasing equality of income distribution, or the degree of improvement in the lives of the lowest 20 per cent of income recipients. Furthermore, some may consider the degree to which the population of a country participates in its governance as a relevant indicator of the level of development. As Meier (1989: 6) so aptly observes, the phenomena that people have chosen to denote as economic development 'are very much a matter of what [they value] as the economy's policy goals. And the definition of development inevitably becomes a "persuasive definition", implying that development – so defined – is a desirable objective.'

But several of the indicators of development besides per capita income growth are beyond the direct influence of MNCs in their production activities. Like other private-sector firms, their primary aim is to earn as much profit as they can through the choice of production, management, and marketing techniques in response to known costs of inputs. Thus, whether their activities promote greater equality of income distribution or not would have to depend on input costs. To the extent that government taxation and regulatory policies affect input costs, it is to the host country governments that attention must be directed when accounting for the type of income distribution found in a country, not MNCs. The same applies to questions about the kinds of goods and services produced by both local and foreign firms.

On the other hand, neglecting to consider fully the costs and benefits associated with the activities of MNCs can lead to misassessments of their contribution to the economic growth and development of host countries. Thus in Chapter 3, I argue the case for comparative examination of the characteristics of foreign and locally owned firms. Comparing the evidence on techniques of production, including capital–labour ratios, skill mix, elasticities of substitution and scale elasticity of input mix, and relating these to the process of development would provide a more helpful basis for judging the contributions of foreign and local firms.

The comparative assessment also helps recognition of the fact that both foreign and local firms often rely on imports of raw materials, machinery, and equipment. Where there are severe restrictions on their ability to obtain foreign exchange, both types of firms may use the importing process to remit funds abroad through over-invoicing. Alternatively, they could under-invoice their exports. The comparative method of evaluating the contributions of firms may also help appreciation of the fact that it is their own incomes that firms remit abroad. Therefore, besides the portions hidden from taxation, the impact of such remittances on the exchange rate or foreign-exchange reserves of a country are no more harmful to the economy than those produced by other agents, including the government.

Another theoretical source of difficulty in evaluating correctly the contributions of MNCs to the development of host LDCs is the definition of technology and its appropriateness. Too many analysts concentrate on capital–labour ratios and scale when discussing the choice of technology in LDCs. Other aspects of technology, including elasticities of substitution, skill mix and the scale elasticity of input mix are left out. Furthermore, the definition of appropriateness used frequently ignores profitability as a relevant criterion for economic growth. The discussion in Chapter 4 thus shows how taking into account several of the characteristics of technology frequently ignored in the debate over MNCs significantly changes many of the negative conclusions that have been reached over the role of foreign firms in economic development.

I also point out in Chapter 4 the lack of scientific basis for the definition of appropriate products for LDCs, or any country for that matter. Users of this concept claim that certain modern or good quality products are inappropriate for consumption by people living in LDCs, regardless of their individual levels of income or personal preferences. Therefore, they argue that firms that produce such goods, often MNCs, do not contribute to the development of LDCs.

My criticism of this argument is that it permits its proponents to impose their personal judgement on the worth of people in LDCs. There is also no valid basis for believing that the aggregate level of happiness, however measured, would be greater if people in LDCs were denied their preferred choice of products. Furthermore, even if there were any valid basis for criticizing the kinds of products consumed in any country, it is consumers whose choices must be criticized, not the firms who serve their needs or preferences.

Some might respond to my criticism of the appropriate products argument by suggesting that consumers, particularly in LDCs, are not rational in their choice of goods and services. But that response would again be an invocation of a distorted definition in economics. Those who founded classical and neoclassical economics, and who ascribed consumer rationality and sovereignty to individuals in the marketplace, defined rationality as purposive behaviour.[3] They did not mean by the concept, for example, 'the substitution of modern methods of thinking, acting, producing, distributing, and consuming for age-old, traditional practices' (Todaro 1989: 123), as some economists now insist rationality means.[4] The latter definition, among other things, merely provides the excuse for recommending interventionist policies against MNCs and other firms, and denying freedom of choice to individuals in LDCs.

The role of MNCs in promoting exports, particularly that of manufactures from LDCs, is another source of debate. The expectation has been that foreign firms, particularly MNCs, would be leaders in exporting manufactured goods because of their greater knowledge of foreign markets and, perhaps, their favoured tariff position with home governments. The positive growth effect on LDC economies from such export activities is also based on Adam Smith's proposition that international trade promotes economic growth by creating a vent for what could have been surplus output at existing prices. Some critics of MNCs have argued that instead of promoting greater exports of manufactures from LDCs, many foreign firms rather have prevented these countries from doing so. They claim that stifling the export potential of LDCs is part of the global profits pursuit of the parent companies of MNCs.

I point out in Chapter 5 that criticism of the export performance of MNCs arises mainly from the failure to recognize that the different motives or circumstances under which foreign firms invest in other countries determine whether they export their products or not. If a firm engages in production to service a foreign market protected by tariffs, it would hardly be profitable for it to export some of its output. Production under such conditions is usually at a higher unit cost of output, hence less competitive in both price and quality in the world market.

Another reason for the criticism may be the difficulty of distinguishing from most published data on LDC exports which proportions are contributed by foreign firms. Furthermore, it is difficult to obtain information from public sources on why foreign firms locate in LDCs, but it is from such evidence that we can determine the sales orientation of foreign firms: whether they have located abroad in order to take advantage of cheap labour and raw materials to manufacture for export, or whether they have gone abroad to escape import tariffs on their products.

I also dispute the positive link necessarily made between export growth and economic growth which underlies some of the criticisms of MNCs. As is becoming increasingly recognized, unless greater exports are associated with a freer economic system, there is little reason for an economy to experience positive growth as a result of such exports. Indeed, subsidizing export growth could result in a slower overall growth for the economy if such subsidies direct resources into less efficient production.

Finally, I discuss in Chapter 6 the question of whether MNCs or foreign firms are more efficient in the utilization of domestic resources than local firms. Arguments of both defenders and most critics of MNCs suggest an efficiency advantage of foreign firms over their local counterparts. There is not enough evidence to examine all aspects of this argument, but the little there is lends much support to it. Measuring efficiency in terms of the total amount of profits made, foreign firms appear on average to be the most efficient employers of capital (savings). Although private local firms typically earn higher rates of profits before taxes than foreign firms, the latter operate on a much larger scale. Foreign firms also derive much higher productivity from labour than any other group of firms, which for LDCs is a significant contribution. The high labour productivity they obtain, mainly through large-scale production and the efficient use of machinery and equipment, ends up in higher wages for their employees.

Besides any relative technological disadvantages private local firms may have, the higher profit taxes they pay appear to limit their scale of production, hence total profits, relative to those of private foreign firms. Treating both types of firms equally with respect to incentives may minimize the scale–efficiency gap between the two types of firms, but it is doubtful if state-owned firms could compete on efficiency grounds with either private local or foreign ones.

With respect to interpretations of the evidence, dispute over the activities of foreign firms in LDCs appears to have arisen from the inadequacy of relevant data, differences in the degree of aggregation of the data, and differences in the statistical methods employed to test competing hypotheses. It is difficult to find published data which separate foreign firms from multinational corporations, but these firms could be different in several aspects, for example, scale or skill mix at the management level. Many tests also have been conducted using a binary classification of firms: foreign versus local. But results from such classification are often different from those of a three- or five-way classification of ownership which distinguishes local private from state-owned firms, or mixed private foreign and local firms from mixed foreign and state-owned firms. Moreover, not all studies employ the same measurement for such important variables as (physical) capital, scale, labour productivity, or skill mix. Equally serious in producing conflicting conclusions may be the different statistical testing methods employed, including matched-pairs, differences in means, and multiple regressions techniques.

In spite of difficulties with the data and differences in the methods used for testing hypotheses on the behaviour of foreign firms, including multinationals, the preponderance of conclusions reached has been mostly favourable. The tests mostly clear these firms of the negative claims made about their contributions to economic growth and development. There is now much less negative emotion stirred in the debate over the role of foreign firms in LDCs than there was in the 1960s and 1970s. However, this does not mean there is unanimity on the appropriate policy to adopt towards these firms. Scepticism still abounds about the wisdom of allowing foreign firms the freedom to operate in LDC economies without much overseeing by host governments.

Indeed, the debate over the development consequences of MNCs in host LDCs has really been a dispute over policy towards foreign firms. Governments typically feel less encumbered in dealing with locally owned firms. They perceive such firms as being as controllable as any other citizens of the country. Foreign firms, on the other hand, appear to present governments with a complicated regulatory environment because of the fact that their owners could appeal to home governments for intervention on their behalf. For MNCs, their size and sometimes the sophistication of their operations also seem to create an image of unwieldiness for host LDC governments.

From an integration of both the theoretical and empirical insights discussed in the chapters above, we can draw the following policy conclusions. Foreign firms should be treated the same way as private local firms, without special privileges (subsidies, tariff protection, and tax holidays) or restraints. Promotion of any particular type of economic growth or development in a host country is not the primary goal of foreign firms or MNCs. Whatever impact their activities may have on host economies depends mainly on the types of policies host governments adopt towards them.

A firm's contribution to economic growth depends on its demand for local resources, land, land-based products, labour, and capital (savings). Special financial privileges granted to foreign firms may enable them to purchase more of these resources. Such privileges then amount to a redistribution of income from domestic residents in favour of foreign ones. Even where the privileges make possible the hiring of more labour or utilization of other local resources in total, the opportunity cost of such privileges must be recognized. Tax revenues may have been forgone or some investible domestic capital may have been transferred to foreign firms in the form of subsidies.

It may be argued that tax holidays are sometimes necessary to attract foreign firms which will engage in land development or road construction as an ancillary part of their main production activities. Even in such a case, it must be decided whether the ancillary activities are properly in the domain of public expenditures for which it would be worth giving up tax revenues. It must always be borne in mind that few firms undertake any expenditures out of charity. Their owners could hardly stand for such use of their investment capital for long.

On the other hand, restraints imposed on foreign firms simply because they are owned by foreigners may be ill-conceived. Owners of foreign firms need to earn good returns on their investment just as local investors do. Restricting profits repatriation by foreign firms is thus an undue restraint. Furthermore, it has not been proven, neither are there reasonable theoretical basis for believing, that owners of foreign firms are more greedy than those of local firms. Thus, government expenditures aimed especially at detecting under-reported incomes of foreign firms may not be money well spent.

I do not deny the possibility of fraudulent activities by foreign firms with respect to their tax liabilities. My argument is that the same tendencies may exist among locally owned firms. Tax collection authorities must, therefore, be vigilant in dealing with both foreign and local firms, bearing in mind the additional costs and benefits of increased auditing or tax policing. It might even be better to lower corporate incomes taxes across the board and remove restraints on the purchase of foreign exchange for both types of firms if these are the inducements for their attempting to cheat on their tax liabilities or evade regulations.

Some Marxist-Leninists may still view the world as caught up in a struggle between capital and labour, and recognize little benefit to LDCs from foreign direct investment, but most critics of foreign firms, especially MNCs, and governments of LDCs recognize there are significant economic benefits to be derived from the activities of foreign firms. What they may be searching for is knowledge of the extent to which foreign firms could be pushed to create more wealth in host countries through either inducements or restrictions on their activities. My argument is that both inducements and restraints entail costs to host countries which may not be worth the benefits. Recognizing the primary motive of profit-making by both foreign and local firms, and creating an environment of the greatest freedom of private enterprise seem to be the appropriate policies for promoting efficient economic growth and development.

Notes

Chapter one: Introduction

1 See, for example, Murray (1981) and Villamil (1979) for arguments along this line.
2 See Biersteker (1978) for an excellent survey of this literature.
3 For some thoughtful criticisms of elements of these proposals, see Amacher *et al.* (1979). Also see Meier (1984: 757) for more references.
4 The inadequacy stems from the static nature of the theory and the concept of competition employed. I discuss the latter inadequacy in Chapter 2.
5 For a good overview of the evolution of modern welfare economics, see Rima (1986), Chapter 14 or Backhouse (1985), Chapter 24.
6 The proper context is that because all economic agents pursue their own self-interests, governments should not aid or restrain some in favour of others.

Chapter two: The multinational corporation: a type of firm

1 This is partly why the profit-maximization motive of the firm remains directly an unverifiable assumption, though an extremely useful one for economic analysis.
2 Some of these savers buy shares of a firm in the stock market instead of bonds at some promised interest. They are thus not entrepreneurs simply because they risk their capital in the firm.
3 For a detailed description of the structure of the modern corporation and the different management and supervisory functions performed by the top executive and board of directors, see, for example, Fama and Jensen (1983).
4 This literature largely follows the work of Berle and Means (1932). For a history of its impact on economics, law, and public policy, see, for example, Hesson (1983) and Stigler and Friedland (1983). Their accounts also contain criticisms of the logic and lack of empirical relevance of Berle and Means's argument.
5 Also see Demsetz (1983) for a further criticism of the so-called 'agency problem', and affirmation, on the basis of empirical evidence, of the

strong identity of interests between the entrepreneur–management group and the shareholders of the firm, namely, profit maximization.

6   This notion has been incorporated into the internalization theory of the multinational corporation, as will be discussed below.

7   See Coase (1937), p. 389, note 3.

8   Aliber (1970, 1971), for example, emphasizes this aspect of the motivation for international production by MNCs.

9   See, for example, Magee (1981).

10 Such a condition may arise from the fact that some other newly developed products effectively compete away the demand for those embodying the rented knowledge, or sufficiently reduce the revenue from the sale of the 'old' products as to make payment of the rental unprofitable.

11 For a survey of this vast literature, see Caves (1971), Horst (1972), Dunning (1973), Hufbauer (1975), Stevens (1974), Hood and Young (1979), Agarwal (1980) and Rugman (1980). Also see Kojima (1978).

12 These build mainly on the work of Bain (1956) and Hymer (1960).

13 Among the main contributors to this perspective are Hymer (1960, 1979), Kindleberger (1969), Aliber (1970), Johnson (1970), Caves (1971), Vernon (1966, 1971), Sweezy and Magdoff (1972), Dunning (1973) and Barnet and Muller (1974).

14 The inadequacies include the failure of this perspective to recognize that it is in the process of trying to be more efficient that MNCs become large firms within industries, and also invest in R&D, and differentiate their products in order to compete more effectively in the marketplace.

15 Others who themselves have contributed to, or are sympathetic with, the application of the concept of internalization to explain the behaviour of MNCs, are yet not so enthusiastic about Rugman's position. See, for example, Buckley (1983), Casson (1982), Kay (1983), Kindleberger (1984) and Parry (1985), also cited for discussion in Rugman (1986).

16 This builds upon Dunning (1973).

17 McNulty (1968) also contrasts the meaning of competition in classical and neoclassical economics. Also see Stigler (1957) for an historical account.

18 I do not deny or wish to trivialize the important contributions to economic analysis made through the use of the perfect competition model. Rather, I wish to point out its lack of relevance or usefulness in explaining the existence of MNCs.

19 It is worth pointing out that the rivalry conception of competition is increasingly gaining acceptance within the field of industrial organization (e.g. Green 1985, 1987). 'Austrian' economists are ahead of mainstream economics in this regard. See, for example, Kirzner (1973).

Chapter three: The firm in economic development

1 For an extensive discussion of the difference between economic growth and development, and some relevant literature, see Meier (1989: 5–30).
2 Their economies soon ran into financial difficulties, resulting in much less growth and a generally worsened standard of living for the majority. Also see Morawetz (1980), and Jameson and Wilber (1981), for further discussion.
3 One thus needs to be careful not to confuse greater equality of income distribution necessarily with a higher average standard of living. The focus on equity in the definition of development may also credit envy, which underlies many arguments for state action to bring about greater equality of income, with scientific reasoning.
4 This policy is due largely to John Maynard Keynes' mistaken belief that low interest rates, created by a country's central bank through increases in money supply, are necessary to promote investment, hence greater employment and economic growth. See, especially, Keynes (1974). The error of this argument has been recognized, at least within the so-called monetarist macroeconomics (e.g. Friedman 1972). For an explanation of how Keynes came by this error, see Ahiakpor (1989a).
5 In most LDCs, whose money and capital markets are rather undeveloped, long-term borrowing by firms tends to affect much fewer households than it does in the MDCs. The opportunity to buy stocks in MNCs is also absent in many LDCs, although host governments sometimes purchase shares in such enterprises in an attempt to influence their investment decisions. Where interest rates are not allowed to vary in response to credit demand and supply conditions, borrowing by MNCs in host countries may have limited influence on the total supply of savings by households.
6 In equilibrium, the after-tax rate of profit would be equal among all firms in an industry, but total profits would differ according to the scale of operation.
7 I elaborate on this argument in Chapter 4.
8 See, for example, Bos *et al.* (1974), Bergsten *et al.* (1978), Hood and Young (1979) and Meier (1984).
9 This point is emphasized, for example, in Helleiner (1973, 1977, 1979). Also see Little *et al.* (1970).
10 For further discussion, see Bauer (1967, 1971, 1984), Friedman (1968), Myint (1971), Lal (1983), and Ahiakpor (1985a).
11 For a good survey of this literature, see Biersteker (1978). Also see Ahiakpor (1986b).
12 See, for example, Jackman (1982) for a good statistical rebuttal of this argument.
13 But the thrust of several chapters devoted to this issue in Rugman and Eden (1985) is that much of this allegation is unfounded. Also see Vernon (1971, 1972).
14 A problem with this argument is that it is founded more on *a priori*

reason, albeit incomplete, than on empirical evidence. Terms of trade could fall and yet more income may be earned from exports. Furthermore, the price elasticity of demand facing an exporting country is roughly equal to the coefficient of world demand elasticity divided by the share of the country's export in total world supply. Thus the elasticity is usually greater than unity.

15 Griffin (1977), Stewart (1977), and Streeten (1972, 1973) are among those who criticize MNCs on this basis.

16 See, especially, Vernon (1971) and Streeten (1973) for further discussion.

17 But local firms also may engage in transfer pricing as a means of accumulating foreign-exchange reserves abroad when restrictions are imposed on private foreign-exchange transactions by the host government. Within such a regime, it may be hard to distinguish transfer pricing on the part of MNCs and local firms. See, for example, Ahiakpor (1986b).

18 Indeed, it is doubtful if MNCs are as powerful against host LDC governments as some have argued, given the ability of several of these governments to nationalize the investments or take over controlling interests in foreign firms, especially during the 1970s. See, for example, Vernon (1977). Kindleberger (1969) also presents some instructive case history of actions taken against MNCs in LDCs. As he argues, the evidence 'contrasts with the Marxian view that direct investment represents neocolonialism or neo-imperialism and continues to hold formerly dependent territories in thrall despite political independence' (p. 153).

Chapter four: The technology of MNCs and economic development

1 For a further illuminating discussion of this point, see Ishikawa (1972). Forsyth *et al.* (1980) attempt to develop a composite index of technology they call an 'index of technical rigidity', but it still falls short. The index neglects other facets of technology such as skill mix and output elasticity of input mix.

2 An example of the confused, early discussions of technology choice in LDCs is the assertion that 'in many areas [of LDCs] there is not even a technology which can be adapted' (Streeten 1972: 220)

3 For example, Frances Stewart includes among the characteristics of technology, scale, skill mix, management, marketing, and the legal institutions within which firms operate, but she considers machinery developed in industrialized countries as necessarily inappropriate for LDCs because of differences between LDCs and MDCs in institutions and climatic conditions. Her argument denies the possibility of such imported machinery being suitably adapted to conditions in LDCs. See Stewart (1974a,b, esp. pp. 17–20, 1977, especially chapters 1, 3 and 4). Streeten (1972) makes a similar argument.

4 Wide variations in capital–labour ratios may indeed represent different technologies or points on different isoquants located along the same or

different isocosts in a two-factor diagram. But until that hypothesis (existence of different technologies) is explicitly tested and confirmed as, for example, in Leipziger (1976) or Lipsey *et al.* (1978), the analyst may be substituting mere supposition for fact.

5   Stewart (1977: 28–9) presents a version of this argument thus: 'to assume that techniques of varying labour and capital intensity exist which produce the *same* product does not make sense, because the technical developments that have increased investment have also been associated with changed products. This also means . . . that some early techniques which might appear to offer a labour-intensive alternative, are ruled out because they are associated with obsolete products' (emphasis in original). However, McBain (1977: 830) refutes Stewart's claims with data on footwear manufactures in Ethiopia.

6   Leibenstein (1966). He attributes between 7 and 291 per cent increase from such reorganization of work place as plant-layout, material-handling, waste control and payment by results. For a criticism of his analysis, see Stigler (1976).

7   Note the collectivist premise of this definition, focused as it is on the maximization of social, not individual welfare.

8   Although sound economic analysis suggests this criterion of appropriateness, it has only recently been taken seriously by major writers on the issue, particularly, Pack (1981) and Ranis (1981). This trend may reflect a resurgence in the application of valid economic principles to LDCs after decades of attempts to discredit such practice among development economists. See, for example, Bauer (1971, 1984) and Lal (1983) for a discussion of the literature.

9   Also see Edwards (1974: 38) for another emphasis of the point that 'appropriate technology should be profitable.'

10 The Concorde aircraft provides another example. For middle- and high-income people in MDCs, time is a rather scarce resource. However, although Concorde economizes the most on air travel time, its operation does not meet the economic test of appropriateness, that is, profitability. Lack of sufficient demand for the aircraft, therefore, has led manufacturers to cease production of new ones.

11 See, for example, Stewart (1974b) and Griffin (1977). Also see White (1978: 36).

12 Cooper (1972/73: 12) credits Frances Stewart with being 'mainly responsible for developing the notion of "inappropriate products",' that is, superior quality products that (allegedly) are not consumed by the poor in LDCs.

13 For a less paternalistic stance, see Ranis (1979), who argues: 'We certainly are not wise enough to preach on the exact nature of the socially optimal choices. All we would argue for is that LDC citizens be given the opportunity of choosing among alternatives, with the fullest possible information and with relative prices more adequately reflecting variations in the quality bundle' (p. 56).

14 In Ahiakpor (1989a), I explain how Keynes confused the relation between savings (capital) and investment, and thus misled many in

economics to concentrate on (aggregate) demand as the main determinant of economic growth.

15 The suggestion that shadow prices must be used as a basis for choosing appropriate technology stems from the recognition that many prices are distorted by government regulations (minimum and maximum prices). Although the correct approach to dealing with price distortions ought to be a call for the removal of government-mandated prices, not the tax-subsidy manipulations often recommended, the free-market approach may be less politically expedient.

16 Stewart (1977: 95) also bases her criticism of Morawetz's shadow-price definition of appropriate technology partly on the ground that there are no unique sets of shadow prices for an economy. However, she fails to extend the same logic to her definition of appropriate products for a country.

17 See, for example, Gillis *et al.* (1987: 138–43).

18 Also see Stewart (1977) for a similar description of 'appropriate' products.

19 Instead of pointing out that it is improper use of the product, including cleaning of bottles and teat, and mixture of the formula that causes the health problems, several writers on this issue have concentrated on blaming the manufacturer for having introduced the product in the first place, or having advertised it as a good alternative to breast-feeding. The Coca-Cola Company, among others, has also been criticized for introducing 'inappropriate', non-nutritious products to LDCs.

20 It is a feeling censured in Judeo-Christian ethics of the Ten Commandments. Thus, the collectivists have no 'godly' basis for their efforts to forcibly bring about equality in the standard of living in LDCs.

21 Also note a fundamental difference between the two feelings of resentment. One arises from a violation of an individual's property rights – the right or freedom to dispose of one's wealth as one chooses – while the other arises from no such violation, but from envy. And there is no tenable argument that people have a natural right to consume that which they have not produced or purchased. It is important not to confuse the biblical call for charity with an assignment of rights to the poor over others' properties. Sen's (1981) arguments on 'entitlements' contain this sort of confusion. He ignores the fact that, besides charity, it is from private incomes that people have legitimate claims to food.

22 On the motives and lifestyles of tourists in LDCs, see Gray (1970), Bryden (1973), MacCannell (1976), Smith (1977) and Kadt (1979).

23 James (1982) actually attempts to defend paternalism towards people in LDCs

24 In fact, inclusion of the source of raw materials among appropriate characteristics of technology is a red herring. Local materials not used in manufacturing can either be consumed or exported. Since it is proceeds from exports that ultimately pay for imports, reliance on imported materials should properly be regarded as one sector's demand

for another's output through international exchange.

25 LDCs covered in the studies include Argentina, Brazil, Chile, Colombia, Ecuador, Ethiopia, Ghana, Hong Kong, India, Indonesia, Kenya, Mexico, Peru, the Philippines, Puerto Rico, Singapore, South Korea, Taiwan, Tanzania, Thailand and Zaire. Industries include food, beverages, chemical products, clothing, electrical and electronic products, footwear, textiles, mining, and automobiles.

26 There is some overlap between the studies surveyed by Waldorf (n.d.) and White (1978).

27 This was the official policy of the government of Ghana in the early 1960s. According to the government, 'an industrialization policy aiming for export had to be (*sic*) capital-expensive policy' (Ghana 1964: 18).

28 In one industry where the difference is statistically significant at the 10 per cent level, foreign firms appear to become more capital-intensive as scale increased.

29 Frequently cited critics of elasticity of substitution estimation include Gaude (1981) and Morawetz (1974, 1976). Also see White (1978: 33).

30 These results were obtained from using the value of fixed assets per production worker as the dependent variable. But using value added per production worker as the dependent variable produced no significant differences in the elasticities of substitution for foreign and local firms at the 5 per cent level. However, at the 10 per cent level of significance, the estimated elasticities appear higher for foreign firms in four industries. See Ahiakpor (1981: 168–70.)

31 Riedel (1975) defines import dependence as 'imported raw materials and intermediate inputs as a percent of the total', while Biersteker (1978) uses the 'percentage of imported materials used in production'.

32 See Ahiakpor (1986b) and Vaitsos (1976), especially appendix tables 15–23.

33 This may also explain the greater concentration of foreign firms in industries relying heavily on imported raw materials for processing. For example, Ahiakpor (1981: 148) estimates a Spearman rank-order correlation of 0.69, significant at the 0.23 per cent level, between average industry dependence on imported materials and the (unweighted) ratio of foreign firms among industries.

34 Attempts by the government of Ghana to implement such a policy in 1982/83 led to considerable reduction in production and worker lay-offs by several firms. The policy was subsequently abandoned. See Ahiakpor (1985b).

Chapter five: Multinational corporations, LDC exports and development

1 See, for example, Cable and Persaud (1987) for descriptions of some of these zones, particularly in Asia.

2 However, Ram (1985) uses a multiple regression/production function approach. Other studies confirming a positive relation between exports and national income growth include Balassa (1978), Krueger (1978),

Tyler (1981) and Kavoussi (1984).

3 For excample, employing dummies to capture the difference between middle- and low-income LDCs, Ram (1985) obtains negative coefficients for low-income countries. But the coefficients are neither statistically significant nor large enough to dominate the positive effect of exports estimated for the pooled sample. Ram (p. 420) thus concludes, exports have 'a much smaller impact . . . on economic growth in the low-income LDCs'. But he later obtains negative coefficients for the export variable when he performs similar tests individually for several low-income LDCs (Ram 1987).

4 Negative correlations between exports and national income growth have been observed also for such notable world export countries as Argentina, Brazil, and Mexico, but whose shares of exports in national income are less than 10 per cent.

5 Also see Bhagwati and Brecher (1980, 1986), and Diaz-Alejandro (1970: 325–6).

6 Lall and Streeten (1977: 135) also claim that they stated their 'inferences about transnationality and origin of control . . . carefully and with qualification because the evidence does not seem strong enough to suggest that either of them actually *causes* lower exports'. Yet they go on to argue that their inferences 'support the argument that foreign investors tend to inhibit exports, owing to the exigencies of their global restriction'.

7 But for Australian firms, 'expected growth of the local [Malaysian] market' was still the most important reason for investing abroad (Ariff and Lim 1987: 106).

8 This is in terms of the opportunity cost of resources committed to production. Thus even if a domestic producer is more efficient than a foreigner in a particular item, it may yet increase both parties' incomes to specialize according to their relative efficiencies in production.

Chapter six: Multinationals and efficiency in resource utilization

1 See, for example, Bosworth (1979) for a discussion of the theoretical difficulties associated with interpreting results based on this approximation of the flow of capital services.

2 Some studies have also used the profit function as an indirect method of estimating total factor productivity (e.g. Levy 1981).

3 Some others have estimated higher profits for foreign firms (e.g. Agarwal 1979).

4 Blomstrom (1988) also finds significantly higher labour productivity among foreign firms compared with local Mexican firms, using a larger data base. Raynauld (1972) and Globerman (1979) also confirm the same differences among US and Canadian firms.

5 Dunning refers to the firms I call multinational corporations (MNCs), as multinational enterprises (MNEs).

Chapter seven: Summary and conclusions

1 My definition of neoclassical economists includes writers between 1870 and 1930. This is in contrast with Keynes' distorted history of economics in which he included writers up to the 1930s among 'classical economists' (Keynes 1974: 3n);

2 'Austrian' economists largely have adopted this practice, which greatly increases the effectiveness of their analysis of market behaviour (see, for example, Kirzner 1973).

3 Thus, explained Alfred Marshall (1964), economics is the study of that aspect of life 'in which man's conduct is most deliberate, and in which he most often reckons up the advantages and disadvantages of any particular action before he enters on it' (p. 17), adding, 'there is scarcely any motive so fitful and irregular' that it could not be analysed within some laws of human behaviour 'by the aid of wide and patient observation' (p. 20).

4 Arguing in a similar vein, Myrdal (1957: 100) also claimed people of LDCs 'have not inherited the traditions of rationality . . . so important in the earlier history of the now-developed countries'. Thus, he believed models of rational choice in neoclassical economics are not applicable to LDCs.

Bibliography

Agarwal, J.C. (1979) 'Productivity of foreign and domestic firms in Indian industries', *Weltwirtschaftliches Archiv* 115 (1): 116–27.

Agarwal, J.C. (1980) 'Determinants of direct foreign investment: A survey', *Weltwirtschaftliches Archiv* 116 (4): 739–73.

Ahiakpor, James C.W. (1981) 'The role of foreign direct investment in manufacturing industry development: The case of Ghana', Unpublished PhD dissertation, University of Toronto.

Ahiakpor, James C.W. (1985a) 'On the irrelevance of neoclassical economics to LDCs: A clarification of some definitions', Department of Economics, Saint Mary's University, Halifax (mimeo).

Ahiakpor, James C.W. (1985b) 'The success and failure of dependency theory: The experience of Ghana', *International Organization* 39 (3): 533–52.

Ahiakpor, James C.W. (1986a) 'The capital intensity of foreign, private local and state owned firms in a less developed country', *Journal of Development Economics*, 20 (1): 145–62.

Ahiakpor, James C.W. (1986b) 'The profits of foreign firms in a less developed country: Ghana', *Journal of Development Economics* 22 (2): 321–35.

Ahiakpor, James C.W. (1989a) 'On Keynes's misinterpretation of "capital" in the classical theory of interest', Working Paper no. 57, Department of Economics, Saint Mary's University, Halifax. (Also forthcoming in the *History of Political Economy*.)

Ahiakpor, James C.W. (1989b) 'Do firms choose inappropriate technology in LDCs?', *Economic Development and Cultural Change* 37 (3): 557–71.

Aliber, R.Z. (1970) 'A theory of direct foreign investment', in C.P. Kindleberger (ed.) *The International Corporation*, Cambridge, MA: MIT Press.

Aliber, R.Z. (1971) 'The multinational enterprise in a multiple currency world', in John H. Dunning (ed.) *The Multinational Enterprise*, London: Allen & Unwin.

Amacher, Ryan C., Haberler, Gottfried, and Willet, Thomas D. (1979) *Challenges to a Liberal Economic Order*, Washington, DC: American Enterprise Institute.

Ariff, M. and Lim, C.P. (1987) 'Foreign investments in Malaysia', in V. Cable and B. Persaud (eds) *Developing with Foreign Investment*, London: Commonwealth Secretariat and Croom Helm.

Backhouse, Roger (1985) *A History of Modern Economic Analysis*, New York: Basil Blackwell.

Bain, J.S. (1956) *Barriers to New Competition*, Cambridge, MA: Harvard University Press.

Balassa, B. (1978) 'Exports and economic growth: Further evidence', *Journal of Development Economics* 5 (2) 181-9.

Balassa, B. (1988) 'The lessons of East Asian development: An Overview', *Economic Development and Cultural Change* 36 (3): S274-90.

Baran, P. and Sweezy, P. (1966) *Monopoly Capitalism*, New York: Monthly Review Press.

Baranson, Jack (1978) *Technology and the Multinational*, Lexington: Lexington Books.

Barnet, R.S. and Muller, R.E. (1974) *Global Reach: The Power of Multinational Corporations*, New York: Simon & Schuster.

Bator, F.M. (1957) 'The simple analytics of welfare maximization', *American Economic Review* 47 (1): 351-92.

Bauer, P.T. (1967) *Economic Analysis and Policy in Underdeveloped Countries*, London: Cambridge University Press.

Bauer, P.T. (1971) *Dissent on Development: Studies and Debates in Development Economics*, London: Weidenfeld & Nicolson.

Bauer, P.T. (1984) *Reality and Rhetoric*, Cambridge, MA: Harvard University Press.

Bell, Clive (1972/73) 'The acquisition of agricultural technology: Its determinants and effects', *Journal of Development Studies* 9: 123-59.

Bennett, Douglas and Sharpe, Kenneth E. (1979a) 'Transnational corporations and the political economy of export promotion: The case of the Mexican automobile corporations', *International Organization* 33 (2): 177-201.

Bennett, Douglas and Sharpe, Kenneth E. (1979b) 'Agenda setting and bargaining power: The Mexican state vs. transnational automobile corporations', *World Politics* 32 (1): 57-89.

Bergsten, C.F., Horst, T., and Moran, T.H. (1978) *American Multinationals and American Interests*, Washington, DC: Brookings Institute.

Berle, Adolf A. and Means, Gardiner C. (1932) *The Modern Corporation and Private Property*, New York: Macmillan.

Bhagwati, J.N. and Brecher, R.A. (1980) 'National welfare in an open economy in the presence of foreign-owned factors of production', *Journal of International Economics* 10 (1): 103-15.

Bhagwati, J.N. and Brecher, R.A. (1986) 'Extending free trade to include international investment: a welfare-theoretic analysis' in S. Lall and Frances Stewart (eds) *Theory and Reality in Development*, London: Macmillan.

Biersteker, T.J. (1978) *Distortion or Development?: Contending Perspectives on the Multinational Corporation*, Cambridge, MA: MIT Press.

Blomqvist, A.G. (1976) 'Empirical evidence on the two-gap hypothesis: A revised analysis', *Journal of Development Economics* 3 (2): 181–93.

Blomstrom, Magnus (1988) 'Labour productivity differences between foreign and domestic firms in Mexico', *Research Paper* no. 6341, Ekonomiska Forskningsinstitutet vid Handelshogskolan, Stockholm, March.

Boon, G.K. (1975) 'Technological choice in metalworking, with special reference to Mexico', in A.S. Bhalla (ed.) *Technology and Employment in Industry*, Geneva: ILO.

Bornschier, Volker (1980) 'Multinational corporations and economic growth', *Journal of Development Economics*, 7 (2): 191–210.

Bos, H.C., Sanders, M., and Seechi, C. (1974) *Private Foreign Investment in Developing Countries*, Boston: D. Reidel.

Bosworth, Derek L. (1979) 'Capital stock, capital services and the use of fuel', in K.D. Patterson and Kerry Schott (eds) *The Measurement of Capital: Theory and Practice*, New York: Holmes & Meier.

Brecher, R.A. and Diaz-Alejandro, Carlos (1977) 'Tariffs, foreign capital and immiserizing growth', *Journal of International Economics* 7 (4): 317–22.

Bruton, H.J. (1969) 'The two-gap approach to aid and development', *American Economic Review* 59 (3): 439–46.

Bryden, John M. (1973) *Tourism and Development: A Case Study of the Commonwealth Caribbean*, Cambridge: Cambridge University Press.

Buckley, Peter J. (1983) 'New theories of international business: Some unresolved issues', in Mark C. Casson (ed) *The Growth of International Business*, London: Allen & Unwin.

Buckley, P.J. and Casson, Mark (1976) *The Future of the Multinational Enterprise*, London: Longman.

Cable, V. and Persaud, B. (1987) *Development with the Multinational Corporation*, London: Commonwealth Secretariat and Croom Helm.

Casson, Mark C. (1982) 'Transaction costs and the theory of the multinational enterprise', in Alan M. Rugman (ed.) *New Theories of the Multinational Enterprise*, London and Basingstoke: Macmillan.

Caves, R.E. (1971) 'International corporations: The industrial economics of foreign investment', *Economica* 38: 1–27.

Chee, P.L. (1980) 'MNCs and the choice of technology: A Malaysian case study', paper presented at the Council for Asian Manpower Studies Workshop, Pattaya, Thailand, April.

Chen, Edward K.Y. (1983a) 'Factor proportions of foreign and local firms in developing countries', *Journal of Development Economics* 12 (1–2): 267–74.

Chen, Edward K.Y. (1983b) *Multinational Corporations, Technology and Employment*, New York: St Martin's Press.

Chenery, H.B. and Strout, A.M. (1966) 'Foreign assistance and economic development', *American Economic Review* 56 (4): 680–733.

Cheung, Steven N.S. (1983) 'The contractual nature of the firm', *Journal of Law and Economics* 26 (1): 1–21.

Clower, R. *et al.* (1966) *Growth Without Development: An Economic*

Survey of Liberia, Evanston: Northwestern University Press.

Coase, R.H. (1937) 'The nature of the firm', *Economica* 4: 386–405.

Cohen, B.I. (1973) 'Comparative behavior of foreign and domestic export firms in a developing economy', *Review of Economics and Statistics* 55 (2): 190–7.

Cohen, B.I. (1975) *Multinational Firms and Asian Exports*, New Haven: Yale University Press.

Cooper, Charles (1972/73) 'Science, technology and production in the underdeveloped countries: An introduction', *Journal of Development Studies* 9: 1–18.

Cooper, Charles (1973) 'Choice of techniques and technological change as problems in political economy', *International Social Science Journal* 25: 293–304.

Cooper, Charles (1982) 'Sectoral capital intensities', in Frances Stewart and Jeffrey James (eds) *The Economics of New Technology in Developing Countries*, London and Boulder: Frances Pinter and Westview Press.

Corbo, Vittorio and Havrylyshyn, Oli (1982) 'Production technology differences between Canadian-owned and foreign-owned firms using translog-production functions', *Working Paper* no. 981, National Bureau of Economic Research, Cambridge, MA.

de la Torre, J. (1974) 'Foreign investment and export dependency', *Economic Development and Cultural Change* 23 (1): 133–50.

Diaz-Alejandro, Carlos F. (1970) 'Direct foreign investment in Latin America', in Charles P. Kindleberger (ed.) *The International Corporation: A Symposium*, Cambridge, MA: MIT Press.

Diaz-Alejandro, Carlos F. (1977) 'Foreign direct investment by Latin Americans', in T. Agmon and C.P. Kindleberger (eds) *Multinational Firms From Small Countries*, Cambridge, MA: MIT Press.

Demsetz, Harold (1983) 'The structure of ownership and the theory of the firm', *Journal of Law and Economics*, 26 (2): 375–90.

Dos Santos, T. (1970) 'The structure of dependence', *American Economic Review* 60 (2): 231–6.

Dunning, J.H. (1973) 'The determinants of international production', *Oxford Economic Papers* 25 (3): 289–336.

Dunning, J.H. (1977) 'Trade, location of economic activity and the MNE: A search for an eclectic approach', in B. Ohlin, P.O. Hesselborn, and P.M. Wijkman, (eds) *The International Allocation of Economic Activity*, New York: Holmes & Meier.

Dunning, J.H. (1981) *International Production and the Multinational Enterprise*, London: Allen & Unwin.

Dunning, J.H. and Rugman, A.M. (1985) 'The influence of Hymer's dissertation on the theory of foreign direct investment', *American Economic Review* 75 (2): 228–32.

Edwards, Edgar O. (1974) *Employment in Developing Nations*, New York: Columbia University Press.

Emery, Robert F. (1967) 'The relation of exports and economic growth', *Kyklos* 20: 470–84.

Evans, P.B. (1972) 'National autonomy and economic development on multinational corporations in poor countries', in R.O. Keohane and J.S. Nye (eds) *Transnational Relations and World Politics*, Cambridge, MA: Harvard University Press.

Fajnzylber, Fernando and Martinez-Tarrago, Trinidad (1976) *Las Empresas Transnacionales*, Mexico City: Fundo De Cultura Economica.

Fama, Eugene F. and Jensen, M.C. (1983) 'Separation of ownership and control', *Journal of Law and Economics* 26 (2): 301-25.

Fong, P.E. (1987) 'Foreign investment and the state in Singapore', in V. Cable and B. Persaud (eds) *Developing with the Multinational Corporation*, London: Commonwealth Secretariat and Croom Helm.

Forsyth, David J.C. and Solomon, Robert F. (1977) 'Choice of technology and nationality of ownership in manufacturing in a developing country', *Oxford Economic Papers* 29 (2): 258-82.

Forsyth, David J.C., McBain, Norman S., and Solomon, Robert F. (1980) 'Technical rigidity and appropriate technology in less developed countries', *World Development* 8 (5/6): 371-98.

Fransman, Martin (1986) *Technology and Economic Development*, Boulder: Westview Press.

Friedman, Milton (1968) *Dollars and Deficits*, New Jersey: Prentice-Hall.

Friedman, Milton (1972) 'Factors affecting the level of interest rates' in John T. Boorman and Thomas M. Havrilesky (eds) *Money Supply, Money Demand, and Macroeconomic Models*, Boston: Allyn & Bacon.

Gaude, J. (1981) 'Capital-labour substitution possibilities: A review of empirical evidence', in A.S. Bhalla (ed.) *Technology and Employment in Industry*, Geneva: ILO.

Gershenberg, I. (1976) 'The performance of multinational and other firms in economically less-developed countries: A comparative analysis of Ugandan data', *Discussion Paper* no. 234, Institute of Development Studies, Nairobi.

Ghana (1964) *Seven Year Development Plan: 1963/64 - 1969/70*, Accra: The Planning Commission.

Gillis, Malcolm, *et al.* (1987) *Economics of Development* (2nd edn), New York: W.W. Norton.

Globerman, S. (1979) 'Foreign direct investment and "spillover" efficiency benefits in Canadian manufacturing industry', *Canadian Journal of Economics* 12 (1): 42-56.

Goncalves, R. and Richtering, J. (1987) 'Intercountry comparison of export performance and output growth', *Developing Economies* 25 (1): 3-18.

Gray, Peter H. (1970) *International Trade - International Travel*, Lexington: D.C. Heath.

Green, Christopher (1985) *Canadian Industrial Organization and Policy*, (2nd edn), Toronto: McGraw-Hill Ryerson.

Green, Christopher (1987) 'Industrial organization paradigms, empirical evidence, and the case for competition policy', *Canadian Journal of Economics* 20 (3): 482-505.

Griffin, Keith (1977) 'Multinational corporations and basic needs development', *Development and Change* 8: 61-76.

Grosse, Robert E. (1985) 'An imperfect competition theory of the MNE',

Journal of International Business Studies 16 (1): 57–80.

Helleiner, G.K. (1973) 'Manufacturing for export, multinational firms and economic development', *World Development* 2 (7): 13–21.

Helleiner, G.K. (1977) 'Transnational enterprises and the new political economy of US trade policy', *Oxford Economic Papers* 29 (1): 102–16.

Helleiner, G.K. (1979) 'Manufactured exports from less developed countries', in W.R. Cline (ed.) *Policy Alternatives for a New International Economic Order*, New York: Praeger.

Helleiner, G.K. (1988) 'Direct foreign investment and manufacturing for export in developing countries: A review of the issues', in Sidney Dell, *Policies for Development*, New York: Macmillan.

Hesson, Robert (1983) 'The modern corporation and private property: A reappraisal', *Journal of Law and Economics* 26 (2): 273–89.

Hood, N. and Young, S. (1979) *The Economics of Multinational Enterprise*, London: Longman.

Horst, T. (1972) 'Firm and industry determinants of the decision to invest abroad: An empirical study', *Review of Economics and Statistics* 54 (3): 258–66.

Hufbauer, G.C. (1975) 'The multinational corporation and direct investment', in Peter B. Kenen (ed.) *International Trade and Finance*, London: Cambridge University Press.

Hughes, H. and You, Poh Seng (1969) *Foreign Investment and Industrialization in Singapore*, Canberra: Australian National University Press.

Hymer, Stephen (1960) *The International Operations of National Firms: A Study of Direct Foreign Investment* (doctoral dissertation published in 1976 by the MIT Press).

Hymer, Stephen (1976) *The International Operation of National Firms: A Study of Direct Foreign Investment*, Cambridge, MA: MIT Press.

Hymer, Stephen (1979) *The Multinational Corporation: A Radical Approach*, Cambridge: Cambridge University Press.

Ingham, Barbara (1979) 'Vent for surplus reconsidered with Ghanaian evidence', *Journal of Development Studies* 15 (3): 19–37.

Ishikawa, S. (1972) 'A note on the choice of technology in China', *Journal of Development Studies* 9: 161–5.

Iyanda, O. and Bello, J.A. (1979) 'Employment effects of multinational enterprises in Nigeria', research on employment effects of multinational enterprises, *Working Paper* no. 10, ILO, Geneva.

Jackman, R.W. (1982) 'Dependence on foreign investment and economic growth in the Third World', *World Politics* 34, (2): 175–96.

James, Jeffrey (1982) 'Product standards in developing countries', in Frances Stewart and J. James (eds) *The Economics of New Technology in Developing Countries*, London and Boulder: Frances Pinter and Westview Press.

James, Jeffrey and Stewart, Frances (1982) 'New products: A discussion of the welfare effects of the introduction of new products in developing countries', in Frances Stewart and J. James (eds) *The Economics of New Technology in Developing Countries*, London and Boulder: Frances Pinter and Westview Press.

Jameson, Kenneth P. and Wilber, Charles K. (1981) 'Socialism and development: Editors' introduction', *World Development* 9 (9/10): 803–11.

Jo, Sung-Hwan (1976) 'The impact of multinational firms on employment and incomes: The case of South Korea', *World Employment Programme Research Working Papers* WEP2-28; WP12, International Labour Office, Geneva.

Johnson, H.G. (1967) 'The possibility of income loss from increased efficiency or factor accumulation in the presence of tariffs', *Economic Journal* 77: 151–4.

Johnson, H.G. (1970) 'The efficiency and welfare implications of the international corporation', in C.P. Kindleberger (ed.) *The International Corporation*, Cambridge, MA: MIT Press.

Johnson, H.G. (1975) *Technology and Economic Interdependence*, London: Macmillan.

Kadt, de Emanuel (1979) *Tourism: Passport to Development?*, New York: Oxford University Press.

Kavoussi, R.M. (1984) 'Export expansion and economic growth: Further empirical evidence', *Journal of Development Economics* 14 (1-2): 241–50.

Kay, Neil M. (1983) 'Multinational enterprise: A review article', *Scottish Journal of Political Economy* 30 (3): 304–12.

Keynes, John M. (1974) *The General Theory of Employment, Interest and Money*, [1936] (paperback), London and Basingstoke: Macmillan.

Kindleberger, C.P. (1969) *American Business Abroad*, New Haven: Yale University Press.

Kindleberger, C.P. (1970) *The International Corporation: A Symposium*, Cambridge, MA: MIT Press.

Kindleberger, C.P. (1984) *Multinational Excursions*, Cambridge, MA: MIT Press.

Kindleberger, C.P. and Audretsch, D.B. (1983) *The Multinational Corporation in the 1980s*, Cambridge, MA: MIT Press.

Kirzner, I.M. (1973) *Competition and Entrepreneurship*, Chicago: The University of Chicago Press.

Kojima, K. (1978) *Direct Foreign Investment*, London: Croom Helm.

Kravis, Irving B. (1970) 'Trade as a handmaiden of growth: Similarities between the nineteenth and twentieth centuries', *Economic Journal* 80: 870–2.

Krueger, A. (1978) *Foreign Trade Regimes and Economic Development: Liberalization Attempts and Consequences*, New York: National Bureau of Economic Research.

Krueger, A. (1980) 'Trade policy as an input to development', *American Economic Review* 70 (2): 288–92.

Lal, Deepak (1975) *Appraising Foreign Investment in Developing Countries*, London: Heinemann.

Lal, Deepak (1983) *The Poverty of 'Development Economics'*, London: Hobart Paperback, No. 16.

Lall, S. (1975) *Foreign Private Manufacturing Investment and Multinational*

Corporations: An Annotated Bibliography, New York: Praeger.

Lall, S. (1976) 'The patent system and the transfer of technology to less developed countries', *Journal of World Trade Law* 10: 1–16.

Lall, S. (1980) 'Monopolistic advantages and foreign involvement by U.S. manufacturing industry', *Oxford Economic Papers* 32 (1): 102–22.

Lall, S. *et al.* (1983) *The New Multinationals: The Spread of Third World Enterprises*, New York: Wiley.

Lall, S. and Streeten, P. (1977) *Foreign Investment, Transnationals and Developing Countries*, Boulder: Westview Press.

Langdon, S.W. (1975) 'Multinational corporations, taste transfer and underdevelopment: A case study from Kenya', *Review of African Political Economy* 2.

Lecraw, D. (1977) 'Direct investment by firms from less developed countries', *Oxford Economic Papers* 29 (3): 442–57.

Lecraw, D. (1979) 'Choice of technology in low-wage countries: A non neo-classical approach', *Quarterly Journal of Economics* 93 (4): 631–54.

Leibenstein, Harvey (1966) 'Allocative efficiency vs. "X-efficiency" ', *American Economic Review* 56 (3): 392–415.

Leipziger, D.M. (1976) 'Production characteristics in foreign encalve and domestic manufacturing: The case of India', *World Development* 4 (4): 321–5.

Levy, Victor (1981) 'Total factor productivity, non-neutral technical change and economic growth', *Journal of Development Economics* 8 (1): 93–109.

Lewellen, Wilber G. (1969) 'Management and ownership in the large firms', *Journal of Finance* 24 (2): 299–322.

Lim, David (1977) 'Do foreign companies pay higher wages than their local counterparts in Malaysian manufacturing?' *Journal of Development Economics* 4 (1): 55–66.

Lim, David (1979) 'Scale and technology in Malaysian manufacturing', *Weltwirtschaftliches Archiv* 115 (1): 128–36.

Lipsey, R.E., Kravis, I.B., and Roldan, R.A. (1978) 'Do multinational firms adapt factor proportions to relative factor prices?', *Working Paper* no. 293, National Bureau of Economic Research, New York.

Little, I.M.D. (1972) 'On measuring the value of private direct overseas investment', in G. Ranis, *The Gap Between the Rich and Poor Nations*, London: Macmillan.

Little, I., Scitovsky, T., and Scott, M. (1970) *Industry and Trade in Some Developing Countries: A Comparative Study*, London: Oxford University Press.

MacCannell, Dean (1976) *The Tourist*, New York: Schoken Books.

MacDougall, G.D.A. (1960) 'The benefits and costs of private investment from abroad: A theoretical approach', *Economic Record* 36: 13–35.

Magee, Stephen P. (1977) 'Information and multinational corporations: An appropriate theory of direct foreign investment', in J. Bhagwati (ed.) *The New International Economic Order: The North–South Debate*, Cambridge, MA: MIT Press.

Magee, Stephen P. (1981) 'The appropriability theory of the multinational corporation', *Annals of the American Academy of Political and Social Science* 458: 123–35.

Maizels, Alfred (1968) *Exports and Economic Growth of Developing Countries*, Cambridge: Cambridge University Press.

Marshall, Alfred (1964) *Principles of Economics* (1920) (8th edn), London: Macmillan.

Mason, R.H. (1973) 'Some observations on the choice of technology by multinational firms in developing countries', *Review of Economics and Statistics* 55 (3): 349–55.

McBain, N.S. (1977) 'Developing country product choice: Footwear in Ethiopia', *World Development* 5 (9/10): 829–38.

McManus, J.C. (1972) 'The theory of the multinational firm', in G. Pacquet (ed.) *The Multinational Firm and the Nation State*, Toronto: Collier-Macmillan.

McNulty, P.J. (1968) 'Economic theory and the meaning of competition', *Quarterly Journal of Economics* 82 (4): 639–56.

Meier, Gerald M. (1984) *Leading Issues in Economic Development*, (4th edn), New York: Oxford University Press.

Meier, Gerald M. (1989) *Leading Issues in Economic Development*, (5th edn), New York: Oxford University Press.

Michaely, M. (1977) 'Exports and growth: An investigation', *Journal of Development Economics* 4 (1): 49–53.

Mill, John Stuart (1965) *Collected Works*, J.M. Robson (ed.), Toronto: University of Toronto Press.

Mooney, J. (1982) 'Profit and concentration in Brazil', unpublished PhD Thesis, University of Notre Dame.

Morawetz, D. (1974) 'Employment implications of industrialization in developing countries', *Economic Journal* 84: 491–542.

Morawetz, D. (1976) 'Elasticities of substitution in industry: What do we learn from econometric estimates?', *World Development* 4 (1): 11–13.

Morawetz, D. (1980) 'Economic lessons from some small socialist developing countries', *World Development* 8: 337–69.

Murray, Robin (ed.) (1981) *Multinationals Beyond the Market: Intra-firm Trade and Control of Transfer Pricing*, Brighton: Harvester Press.

Myint, H. (1958) 'The classical theory of international trade and the underdeveloped countries', *Economic Journal* 68: 317–37.

Myint, H. (1971) *Economic Theory and Underdeveloped Countries*, New York: Oxford University Press.

Myrdal, Gunnar (1957) *Economic Theory and Underdeveloped Regions*, New York: Harper & Row.

Natke, P.A. (1985) 'Transfer pricing by MNE's in Brazilian manufacturing industries', in A.M. Rugman and L. Eden, (eds) *Multinationals and Transfer Pricing*, London: Croom Helm.

Newfarmer, Richard S. (1983) 'Multinationals and marketplace magic in the 1980's', in Charles Kindleberger and David Audretsch (eds) *The Multinational Corporation in the 1980's*, Cambridge, MA: MIT Press.

Newfarmer, Richard S. and Marsh, Lawrence (1981) 'Foreign ownership market structure and industrial performance: Brazil's electrical industry',

Journal of Development Economics 8 (1): 47–75.

Ohlin, B., Hesselborn, P. and Wijkman, P. (1977) *The International Allocation of Economic Activity*, New York: Holmes & Meier.

Pack, Howard (1979) 'Technology and employment: Constraints on optimal performance', in S.M. Rosenblatt (ed.) *Technology and Economic Development: A Realistic Perspective*, Boulder: Westview Press.

Pack, Howard (1981) 'Appropriate industrial technology: Benefits and obstacles', *Annals of the American Academy of Political and Social Science* 458: 27–40.

Pack, Howard (1984) 'Productivity and technical choice: applications to the textile industry', *Journal of Development Economics* 16 (1–2): 153–76.

Panchareon, W. (1980) 'Multinational corporations and host country technology: Thailand', paper presented at the Council for Asian Manpower Studies Workshop, Pattaya, Thailand, April.

Parry, Thomas G. (1985) 'Industrialization as a general theory of foreign direct investment: A critique', *Weltwirtschaftliches Archiv* 121 (3): 564–9.

Perkins, F.C. (1983) 'Technology choice, industrialization and development experiences in Tanzania', *Journal of Development Studies* 19 (2): 213–43.

Pickett, James, Forsyth, D.J.C., and McBain, N.S. (1974) 'The choice of technology, economic efficiency and employment in developing countries', *World Development* 2 (3): 47–54.

Pickett, James and Robson, R. (1977) 'A note on operating conditions and technology in African textile production', *World Development* 5 (9/10): 879–82.

Possas, M.L. (1979) 'Employment effects of multinational enterprises in Brazil', Research on Employment Effects of Multinational Enterprises, *Working Paper* no. 7, International Labour Office, Geneva.

Ram, R. (1985) 'Exports and economic growth: Some additional evidence', *Economic Development and Cultural Change* 33 (2): 415–25.

Ram, R. (1987) 'Exports and economic growth in developing countries: Evidence from time-series and cross-section data', *Economic Development and Cultural Change* 36 (1): 51–72.

Ranis, Gustav (1973) 'Industrial sector labour absorption', *Economic Development and Cultural Change* 21 (3): 387–408.

Ranis, Gustav (1979) 'Appropriate technology: Obstacles and opportunities', in S.M. Rosenblatt, (ed.) *Technology and Economic Development: A Realistic Perspective*, Boulder: Westview Press.

Ranis, Gustav (1981) 'Technology choice and the distribution of income', *Annals of the Academy of Political and Social Science* 458: 41–53.

Raynauld, Andre (1972) 'The ownership and performance of firms', in Gilles Pacquet (ed.) *The Multinational Firm and the Nation State*, Toronto: The Ryerson Press.

Riedel, J. (1975) 'The nature and determinants of export-oriented direct foreign investment in a developing country: A case study of Taiwan', *Weltwirtschaftliches Archiv* 111 (3): 505–26.

Reuber, Grant L. (1973) *Private Foreign Investment*, Oxford: Clarendon Press.

Rima, Ingrid H. (1986) *Development of Economic Analysis* (4th edn), Homewood: Irwin.

Robbins, Sidney M. and Stobaugh, Robert B. (1973) *Money in the Multinational*, New York: Basic Books

Rosenblatt, S.M. (1979) *Technology and Economic Development: A Realistic Perspective*, Boulder: Westview Press.

Rosenthal, Gert (1973a) 'The expansion of the transnational enterprise in Central America: Acquisition of domestic firms', (mimeo).

Rosenthal, Gert (1973b) 'The role of private foreign investment in the development of the Central American Market', unpublished manuscript, cited in S. Lall (1980).

Rugman, A.M. (1980) 'Internalization as a general theory of foreign direct investment: A re-appraisal of the literature', *Weltwirtschaftliches Archiv* 116 (2): 365-79.

Rugman, A.M. (1981) *Inside the Multinationals*, London: Croom Helm.

Rugman, A.M. (1986) 'New theories of the multinational enterprise: An assessment of internalization theory', *Bulletin of Economics Research* 38 (2): 101-18.

Rugman, A.M. and Eden, L. (1985) *Multinationals and Transfer Pricing*, London: Croom Helm.

Schive, C. (1980) 'Multinational corporations and host country technology: A factor proportion approach in Taiwan', paper presented at the Council for Asian Manpower Studies Workshop, Thailand: Pattaya.

Sen, Amartya K. (1981) *Poverty and Famines*, Oxford: Clarendon Press.

Sepulveda, Bernardo and Chumacero, Antonio (1973) *La Inversion Extranjero en Mexico*, cited in Waldorf (n.d.).

Sharma, Basu (1984) 'Multinational corporations and industrialization in Southeast and East Asia', *Contemporary Southeast Asia* 6 (2): 159-71.

Schumpeter, J.A. (1955) *The Theory of Economic Development*, Cambridge, MA: Harvard University Press.

Smith, Adam (1976) *The Wealth of Nations* (1776), (Cannan ed.), Chicago: University Press.

Smith, Valene L. (1977) *Hosts and Guests: The Anthropology of Tourism*, Pennsylvania: University of Pennsylvania Press.

Soediyono (1980) 'Multinational corporations and host country technology: A case study of Indonesia', paper presented at the Council for Asian Manpower Studies Workshop, Pattaya, Thailand, April.

Sourrouille, Juan V. (1976) 'The impact of transnational enterprises on employment and income: The case of Argentina', ILO World Employment Programme, *Research Working Paper*, WP 7, ILO, Geneva.

Stevens, G.V.G. (1974) 'The determinants of investment', in J.H. Dunning (ed.) *Economic Analysis and the Multinational Enterprise*, London: Allen & Unwin.

Stewart, Frances (1972) 'A note on social cost-benefit analysis and class conflict in LDC's', *World Development* 1 (1): 31-9.

Stewart, Frances (1974a) 'Editor's introduction', *World Development* 2 (3): 1-2.

Stewart, Frances (1974b) 'Technology and employment in less developed countries', *World Development* 2 (3): 17-46.

Stewart, Frances (1977) *Technology and Underdevelopment* (2nd edn), London and Basingstoke: Macmillan.

Stewart, Frances and James, Jeffrey (1982) *The Economics of New Technology in Developing Countries*, London and Boulder: Frances Pinter and Westview Press.

Stigler, G.J. (1957) 'Perfect competition, historically contemplated', *Journal of Political Economy* 65 (1): 1–17.

Stigler, G.J. (1976) 'The xistence of X-efficiency', *American Economic Review*, 66.

Stigler, George T. and Friedland, Claire (1983) 'The literature of economics: The case of Berle and Means', *Journal of Law and Economics* 26 (2): 237–68.

Stoever, William A. (1986) 'Foreign investment as an aid in moving from least developed to newly industrializing: A study in Korea', *Journal of Developing Areas* 20 (2): 223–48.

Streeten, P.P. (1972) 'Technology gaps between rich and poor countries', *Scottish Journal of Political Economy* 19: 213–30.

Streeten, P.P. (1973) 'The multinational enterprise and the theory of development policy', *World Development* 1 (10): 1–14.

Streeten, P.P. (1974) 'The theory of development policy', in J.H. Dunning (ed.) *Economic Analysis and the Multinational Enterprise*, London: Allen & Unwin.

Streeten, P.P. and Lall, S. (1973) 'Summary of methods and findings of a study of private foreign investment in six less developed countries', Document no. TD/B/C.3/111, UNCTAD, Geneva.

Sunkel, O. (1972) 'Big business and dependencia: A Latin American view', *Foreign Affairs* 50 (3): 517–31.

Sweezy, P.M. and Magdoff, H. (1972) *The Dynamics of American Capitalism*, New York: Monthly Review Press.

Todaro, Michael P. (1989) *Economic Development in the Third World* (4th edn), New York: Longman.

Tyler, W.G. (1978) 'Technical efficiency and ownership characteristics of manufacturing firms in a developing country: A Brazilian case study', *Weltwirtschaftliches Archiv* 114 (2): 360–78.

Tyler, W.G. (1981) 'Growth and export expansion in developing countries', *Journal of Development Economics* 9 (1): 121–30.

Vaitsos, Constantine V. (1974) *Intercountry Income Distribution and Transnational Enterprises*, Oxford: Clarendon Press.

Vaitsos, Constantine V. (1976) 'The revisions of the international patent system: legal considerations for a Third World position', *World Development* 5, 2: 85–99.

Vaitsos, Constantine V. (1978) 'The role of transnational enterprise in Latin American integration efforts: Who integrates and with whom, how and for whose benefit?' Prepared for UNCTAD Secretariat and presented at Conference on TNCs and Economic Integration, Lima, Peru, June.

Vernon, Raymond (1966) 'International investment and international trade in the product cycle', *Quarterly Journal of Economics* 2 (80): 190–207.

Vernon, Raymond (1971) *Sovereignty at Bay: The Multinational Spread of U.S. Enterprises*, New York: Basic Books.

Vernon, Raymond (1972) *Restrictive Business Practices*, New York: United Nations.

Vernon, Raymond (1975) *Multinational Enterprise in Developing Countries: Analysis of National Policies*, New York: United Nations Industrial Development Organization.

Vernon, Raymond (1977) *Storm Over the Multinationals: The Real Issues*, Cambridge, MA: Praeger.

Villamil, J.J. (1979) *Transnational Capitalism and National Development*, New Jersey: Humanities Press.

Waldorf, W.H. (n.d.) 'Transnational corporations, their impact on labour markets', unpublished manuscript, New York: United Nations Center on Transactional Corporations.

Wanigatunga, R.C. (1987) 'Direct private overseas investment in export oriented ventures: Recent developments in Sri Lanka', in V. Cable and B. Persaud (eds) *Developing with Foreign Investment*, London: The Commonwealth Secretariat and Croom Helm.

Wells, Louis T. (1975) 'Economic man and engineering man: Choice of technology in a low-wage country', in C.P. Timmer *et al.*, *The Choice of Technology in Developing Countries*, Cambridge, MA: Center for International Affairs, Harvard University.

Westphal, Larry, Rhee, Y.W., and Purcell, G. (1979) 'Foreign influences on Korean industrial development', *Oxford Bulletin of Economics and Statistics* 41 (4): 359–88.

White, L.T. (1978) 'The evidence on appropriate factor proportions for manufacturing in less-developed countries: A survey', *Economic Development and Cultural Change* 27 (1): 27–59.

Willmore, L. (1976) 'Direct foreign investment in Central American manufacturing', *World Development* 4 (6): 499–517.

Winston, G.C. (1979) 'The appeal of inappropriate technologies: Self-inflicted wages, ethnic pride and corruption', *World Development* 7 (8/9): 835–45.

World Bank (1987) *World Development Report 1987*, New York: Oxford University Press.

Worrell, D. *et al.* (1987) 'Private foreign investment in Barbados', in V. Cable and B. Persaud (eds) *Developing with the Multinational Corporation*, London: Commonwealth Secretariat and Croom Helm.

Index

For Product Safety Concerns and Information please contact our EU
representative GPSR@taylorandfrancis.com Taylor & Francis Verlag GmbH,
Kaufingerstraße 24, 80331 München, Germany

Printed and bound by CPI Group (UK) Ltd, Croydon, CR0 4YY
12/05/2025
01867598-0002